The United
States of Trump

The United States of Trump

THE INDEPENDENT GUIDE TO
THE DONALD TRUMP PHENOMENON
AND THE GENERAL ELECTION

———

Bernhard Klee

© 2016 by Bernhard Klee, Yeah LLC
The Library of Congress has catalogued the hardcover as follows:
Library of Congress Control Number: 2016908950
Bernhard Klee, New Providence, NJ
Manufactured in the United States of America
ISBN: 0692725725
ISBN 13: 9780692725726

To my sons, Vincent and Benjamin.

To our brave members of the military, who sacrifice so much every day to defend this nation and our values around the world.

Contents

Foreword

—

THERE IS STILL DISBELIEF AMONG the so-called political establishment and even shock among many of the country's magazines, newspapers and TV channels about Donald Trump's rise to the Republican nomination. The "self-sorting" of America ensured that many of the same people didn't see the tidal wave coming for a long time and were wondering where the enthusiasm for Donald Trump was coming from. First his supporters were classified as the "Walmart voters," then as angry, un-educated, and supposedly racist white working-class people. Today it is clear that it has become a powerful political movement that covers every socio-demographic group. The commonality among all of them is that they want a non-partisan, non-ideological fixer that can solve problems and run government like a business. They want a focus on immigration, taxes, jobs, the budget deficit and a foreign policy that is coherent and keeps Americans safe. Love him or hate him, "the Donald" seems to make strong impressions on everyone who hears him. The insatiable appetite of the public to watch Trump, and therefore the way the media are outdoing each other in covering Trump, is unprecedented. Nearly $2 billion in free media later, the reality TV star is now the nominee for president of the party of Lincoln and Reagan. Donald Trump has tried before to become president, but somehow 2016 is different; it seems his personality and message match the mood of large swaths of the American electorate.

His campaign is centered on the authenticity of the Trump brand, and his pitch is as simple as it is effective: "Look at my success in life, and look at the situation America is right now in. If you make me your president, I can change our trajectory as a country and make us all winners." Americans across all political spectrums see the lack of common sense in politics today and have had enough of endless partisan debates about dead-end ideological issues. Building a business empire takes hard work, team building, negotiation skills, cost control, marketing and sales skills, innovative ideas, and above all sound judgment. US presidential primaries and the general election are the biggest and also longest showcase of democracy in the world. They are the toughest job interview for the most important job in the world. Yet many have questioned Trump's emotional maturity and self-righteousness to the point of wondering whether he can be presidential, positive and inclusive. He has learned and adapted all of his life, but when will he finally be able to rein himself in and show he can be an empathetic leader? To win in the general election, he has to keep adding new people and demographics to his voting base and not continue to antagonize.

Trump's emergence is a clear reaction to Barack Obama's presidency. His magnetism, flamboyance, hyperbole, transparency and his aggressive style, have channeled the voices of an angry Republican base that feels betrayed and thinks it has no voice. Many of the arguments being made right now were made about Reagan in 1980: that he would be dangerous and unpredictable as a president. America in 2016 is less optimistic and less hopeful than ever, which is unfortunate as optimism and a strong belief in tomorrow are the hallmarks of America. The administration, in its foreign policy, is losing against a band of thugs in Syria terrorizing the world and exporting unrest to Europe and the Middle East while committing the uttermost cruelties against humanity every day in full view of the world. In its domestic policy, it prioritizes social-liberal pet projects over running an effective government, working with Congress, and reducing the ballooning debt. It seems as if taking no risk in the 2016 election could be the biggest risk of all.

I want to provide deeper insights into Donald Trump the politician and his rise in the primaries and where it could lead if he were to become president. Ideally this book will contribute to a richer discussion than the status quo partisan talking points. I want to explain the current trends in America, the issues, the opportunities and provide a different perspective on the Donald Trump campaign. As a marketing professional the marketing story behind his campaign is worth telling and exploring how it may play out in the general election.

As a recently naturalized citizen who immigrated legally I'm excited to be able to vote for the first time. I love political discussions and enjoy our democratic process. In our family we always had heated political discussions around the dinner table. It was normal that our grandfather would challenge everyone's political viewpoint and exciting for me growing up. Despite or maybe because of the emotional and heated discussions we felt more appreciated as individuals and more connected after the discussions. We felt the larger role we play in life beyond just our individual ambitions. In many ways I wish the same for us in our larger American family. After Nov. 8th I hope we take the opportunity to come together and solve our increasingly unaddressed challenges as a more united country.

CHAPTER 1

The Trump Phenomenon Explained

———

A FERTILE GROUND

THE REPUBLICAN PRIMARY SEASON WAS historic, unconventionally dramatic as never before. Starting with maybe the deepest and most diverse field ever, seventeen candidates competed, among them Hispanics, a woman, an African American, a famous doctor, a former CEO of HP, a real estate mogul turned reality TV star, and many governors and senators. Donald Trump was competing against many accomplished political leaders but "his Trump card" was that Republicans wanted an outsider like never before.

As much as his campaign appears off the cuff, he laid the groundwork for his 2016 run over the course of several years. As early as 1987, Trump talked publicly about his desire to run for president. He toyed with mounting a campaign in 2000 on the Reform Party ticket, and again in 2012 as a Republican. Two years later, Trump briefly explored running for governor of New York before setting his sights on the presidential campaign in March 2014.

Throughout 2014, three advisers (Roger Stone, Michael Cohen, and Sam Nunberg) were analyzing the Republican field for Trump. To break out of the pack, he made what appears to be a deliberate decision to be provocative, even outrageous. "If I were totally presidential, I'd be out of the race already", Trump said in an interview with Bill O'Reilly. (1)

Donald Trump waged what was arguably the most effective primary campaign in US history, considering the crowded field of seventeen competitors, most of them politicians and one of them coming from a political dynasty that had already produced two US presidents and had access to the biggest pool of campaign contributions. He has proven to be unrivaled in his ability to forge bonds with a sizable segment of Americans over economic insecurities, cultural change in America, and incompetent or self-centered politicians answering only to special interests and lobbyists.

A large share of American voters are angry today: angry with their own representatives, angry with their opponents, and angry with the world. Let's look a bit closer into the seven factors responsible for Trump's win in the primaries. All of them interacted to give Donald Trump a decisive and unchallenged win.

THE ECONOMY AND POLITICAL GRIDLOCK IN WASHINGTON, DC

"It's the economy, stupid", captured the mood of the electorate during the Bill Clinton campaign in 1992. America went through tough economic times again in 2008, but 2015/2016 felt different. It was coupled with a complete political gridlock. Both parties had grown so hostile toward each other that the president was making policy via executive orders, Republicans resorted to blocking even constitutional moves by the president, keeping the Supreme Court not working rather than accepting a new judge, and even bringing the country to the edge of debt default rather than compromising. While unemployment had gone down, real income for the average American had not gone up in a decade. The key economic indicators were much worse than in 1992, when Ross Perot ran for president as an independent candidate and even led the field in the general election for some time. Voters were fed up with politicians, especially on the Republican side. What a window of opportunity for a businessman and political outsider to run. As globalization and technological transformation left many working-class people behind, they wanted nothing more than to have their voices heard in national politics again instead of being frowned upon by both party establishments. The answer to the question "Do you feel your voice is being heard in politics?" became the number one predictor of Donald Trump voters.

America's optimism has long been one of the biggest differences between the United States and Europe. But for the first time in American history, American's strong optimism was waning as a majority of Americans, 76%, no longer believed that their children would have a better life than they had, the worst result in that survey's history, and the results were similar across race, age, income, and party affiliation. (2)

Other facts were clear as well: ninety-three million Americans were out of the labor force, forty-five million were on food stamps, and the US federal debt had swollen to over $19 trillion debt, over $42,000 for every American, from child to old person. The stats and facts below paint an unfortunate picture:

* Two-thirds of Americans believed that the economy was rigged in favor of the rich.
* Almost 70% believed their politicians didn't care about ordinary Americans.
* *Between 2007 and 2014, the wages of many workers declined; the lowest paid, struggling to adapt to falling demand for low-skilled factory labor, were hit the most. (3)*
* The economic recovery since 2011 had reduced unemployment but incomes had stagnated. Underemployment and the so-called "working poor" are still big issues.
* Young people especially had a harder time finding high-paying jobs, and they had accumulated significant student debt.

* There was the perception that America's dominance in the world was under attack economically and militarily.
* The middle class had been shrinking all across the United States, driven mainly by the decline in manufacturing jobs in the United States, which were being outsourced to China and Mexico.
* In the first decade of this century, those in the middle class actually lost income, and the top 1% came to control more wealth than the bottom 90%.
* GDP growth is still low, only 1.2% growth in Q2 of 2016.

Many Americans asked themselves during the Republican primaries which of the candidates would be the most forceful, daring, and assertive in taking on prominent politicians on both sides to solve the political gridlock in Washington, DC. That's where the outspoken, independent, eccentric real estate mogul and billionaire came in.

Trump sensed the rage that flared from pain in the middle-aged white working class and made it the fuel of his campaign. This is the base of the Republican Party, and it has suffered from globalization, low-wage immigrant labor, and free trade.

Some facts to consider: Republican presidential candidates have received majorities of the white vote in every election since 1964. In 2012, Barack Obama won only 40% of this vote (the average for Democrats in the past half century) and still won the general election based on his strong numbers in other demographics. But no Republican candidate—not even Richard Nixon or Ronald Reagan—made as specific an appeal to the economic anxieties and social resentments of white Americans as Trump has. The white electorate has declined since 1976 from 89% of the American voting public to 72% in 2012 and is 70% in 2016. In the Democratic Party there is also a big division. Hillary Clinton won big with Hispanics and African Americans however Bernie Sanders with younger and better-educated white voters. It will be interesting to see after Bernie Sanders lost to Hillary Clinton in the primaries, whether these voters will revert to the Republican side, stay home, or vote for her after all.

George Packer explains in the article "Head of Class" in *The New Yorker* w hy so many Americans in the so-called heartland are feeling left behind, by the culture and the economy:

Middle-aged white Americans and primarily less-educated ones are economically challenged since the turn of the century but they have also been dying at ever-increasing rates. This declining life expectancy is true of no other age or ethnic group in the United States. The main factors are alcohol, opioids, and suicide, an epidemic of despair. In twenty-one counties across the South and the Midwest, mortality rates among middle-aged white women with lower education have actually doubled since the turn of the century. He comments that they sense the indifference or disdain of the winners on the prosperous East and West Coasts and in the innovative cities, and it is reciprocated. (4)

Charles Murray from the *Wall Street Journal* adds to this analysis another reason for the high appeal of Donald Trump. It comes from the belief in American exceptionalism that this group of voters feels particularly strong about. This belief is characterized by three core values: egalitarianism, liberty, and individualism. These values used to be shared across the political aisle but no longer are. Egalitarianism especially seems to have fallen out of mode with Democrats. At the same time as egalitarianism is no longer an accepted cross-partisan belief, the other two components of American exceptionalism also are under attack: the principles of liberty and individualism. By the beginning of the 1980s, Democratic elites had started subscribing to an ideology in open conflict with liberty and individualism as traditionally understood. This consolidated the Democratic Party's longtime popularity with ethnic minorities, single women, and low-income women, but it alienated another key Democratic constituency: the white working class. America's once-vaunted liberty is now constrained by thousands of petty re-strictions that touch almost anything we do, individualism is rou-tinely ignored in favor of group rights. (5)

THE STATE OF THE REPUBLICAN PARTY AND ITS PERCEPTION AMONG VOTERS

The Republican Party needs time to get used to the fact that Donald Trump has just completed a hostile takeover. The party of Lincoln and Reagan will now be led by a real estate mogul turned reality star turned politician, someone who is seen as ideologically flexible and highly unpredictable. On topics such as international trade deals, the Republican Party and most of its establishment have a different view from Trump's; the same is true for Planned Parenthood, immigration, minimum wage, Social Security and Medicare.

As mentioned before, the Republican Party has failed to show its members and voters any results from the large majority it has in Congress. Based on the Rasmussen Report from February 2016, most voters (61%) believe that Congressmen sell their votes in ex-change for campaign contributions, and only 11% of Americans believe that Congress is doing a good job. The constant gridlock in Washington has frustrated Americans. (6) As of March 2016, the Republican Party reached its highest disapproval rating by the American public since 1992 at 62%; only 33% of Americans saw it favorably. This drop came mainly from a more negative view of Republicans about their party. And a new record of 25% of Americans had an unfavorable view of both parties, the highest since 1992. (7)

The American middle class, which is essential for American democracy, has not benefited as much as in past economic-recovery periods and feels that only the elites get ever richer and politicians no longer have their interests in mind. This perception is strengthened by the Washington stalemate on many topics. Even with a clear Republican majority in both houses, there has never been a Congress that has achieved so little. The *Citizens United* verdict, in which lobbies were granted the right to spend as much money as they please on a candidate of their choosing, has further emboldened that view. Politicians seem to rely more on a few powerful spenders than on individual Americans.

The behavior of many Republicans toward Donald Trump is not helpful but damaging to the Republican Party and their chances in November. Jeb Bush, for example, signed a pledge before the primaries to support the Republican nominee but is now no longer willing to honor that. The same is true for John Kasich who should help to win the most important battleground state, Ohio, but is not supportive contrary to his pledge. Ted Cruz has even misused the Republican convention to voice his dissent. Former Republican nominee Mitt Romney, who Trump supported strongly in 2012, talks still bad about Trump wherever he can.

Donald Trump's critics within the party need to understand that the Republican Party has scorned its own supporters and those voters are now siding with Trump. The Republican Party needs to address its issues; going against the candidate that has won the most primary votes of any Republican candidate will not help. The party tried to marginalize religious and social conservatives who opposed upfront legalization on unauthorized immigrants. Those voters did not give up their stance on immigration and trade deals just because of Republican donors. The Republican primaries of 2016 are the outcome of that: Ted Cruz, Ben Carson, and Trump together got 63% of the vote in polling among Republicans. This is why the Republican establishment's attacks on Trump have proven so ineffective, as it imagines winning elections without the mass of its own voters. It claims the mantle of pragmatism and demands deference even as it adopts wildly unpopular policies. Donald Trump benefited from this as over 60% of Republican voters declare at exit polls that they feel betrayed by their own party. (8)

Donald Trump is however somewhat aligned with the Tea Party movement within the Republican Party. He speaks the Tea party's language, believes in American exceptionalism, and is on the same page with it regarding trade deals, immigration, fewer taxes, an "America First" foreign policy, and also fighting special interests. (9)

Donald Trump's opposition to the Iraq War was very loud, and he even went so far as to say that George W. Bush made a big mistake by going into Iraq. In public rallies he not only beleaguered the American resources lost there (lives of our soldiers, trillions of dollars) but also mourned the millions of Iraqis who lost their lives as a consequence of that war. However, he is not an isolationist just because he wants to rethink or renegotiate our foreign military commitments, as he also wants to destroy ISIS as soon as he will become president.

The Most Crowded Field Ever
There is no question that the most crowded US presidential primary field in the history has helped Donald Trump. His broad name recognition based on being the host of a hit reality TV show helped. He could visibly and metaphorically position all the politicians as a crowd with a similar flaw—"all those politicians, only words, no action"—and set himself apart. Most importantly, the big number of candidates kept many donors and officials on the sidelines for a long time. It created a huge collective-action problem, in which none of the Republican candidates had a clear incentive to attack Trump. By New Hampshire there were still nine, in South Carolina six, and on Super Tuesday still five candidates in the race. The

race narrowed to three candidates only after two-thirds of delegates to the Republican convention had been awarded. It became a one-to-one race only after Trump had effectively secured the nomination.

The 2016 Republican primaries showed that all candidates underestimated Donald Trump to their own peril. The more experienced candidates spent valuable time and money attacking each other as their individual end games involved them versus Trump, in which case they were hoping voters would side with them instead of the perceived irrational choice. The aggregate of those individually smart strategy choices proved detrimental. Trump could stay on top of the field appearing to be presidential or as the "big dog" and outsider larger-than-life figure watching the political pundits attacking each other as they would in Congress or another political arena. This way he was not forced into policy detail early on and could build up his image and perceived leadership role in an undisputed way. Chris Christie blocked Rubio from gaining strength after a successful attack ahead of New Hampshire, which cost them both. After the New Hampshire primary, Christie dropped out, but Rubio had lost valuable time. Rubio and Bush attacked each other for some time, and so did Cruz and Rubio. Jeb Bush was the only candidate attacking Trump early on while Trump resorted to "counterpunching," as he would call it, plus proactively attacking anyone who would rise in the polls (Carly Fiorina, Ben Carson, and Cruz at times).

Every candidate wants to be number one in the polls, but only Donald Trump backed it up with targeted messages that electrified the electorate, got him broad media coverage and forced all of his opponents to react to it. This way he led early in the polls and built his leadership image by owning topics and forcing his game upon his opponents rather letting them develop their own public images on their terms.

His first statement on illegal Mexican immigrants was planned to bring him immediate support from a loyal base and catapulted him to the top of polls within days. His next strategy was to stay on top by either personal attacking the other candidates or, whenever candidates saw a rise in the polls, to launch another unique and powerful message the media had to take up, increasing his media coverage again. Social media served the Trump campaign well in that regard to understand how much chatter was going on at any time and in what mood. His strategy from the beginning was to dominate the topics and therefore the coverage, which he did throughout the campaign. It was first immigration, then trade deals, veterans and the US military, and then the strategy against ISIS and Muslim immigration.

DONALD TRUMP: THE PERSONALITY, THE BRAND, AND THE MEDIA HYPE

The Personality

Donald Trump had a great interest in running for president for a long time. But he always believed somebody else could turn the American government around, and he would not have to jump in the ring himself. Then, after eight years of watching Obama, at age seventy and with his three oldest children having enough experience to manage the company he built, he was ready. As he would say later, he ran because this country was gridlocked and no longer respected internationally, and he thought America needed somebody like him to fix it.

The US presidential primaries are really about personalities and much less about the issues. For a Republican looking for someone different from Obama, there is a stark difference between Donald Trump and Barack Obama. If you are looking for the diametric opposite, it is Trump; he is your manifest anti-Obama in every way.

Obama is a community Organizer; he gives, with a Teleprompter, beautifully crafted speeches. His trademark is his integrity but also his light-hearted way of conducting the presidency; you rarely see him angry or shouting but he tends to moralizing with condescension. He hardly ever gets emotional but likes to stay above the frame like an impartial analyst or bystander commenting on politics. Obama only seems to be emotionally invested on the topics of gun violence, global warming or social liberal agenda topics like marriage equality.

Contrast that with Donald Trump, the real estate developer famous for getting people fired for underperformance on national TV. He is a master salesperson; he is tough, speaks at a fourth-grade level but without a teleprompter and is constantly angry and/or shouting. He uses harsh language, radiates resolve, hard work, grit, and assertiveness. He mirrors the mood of his voters and is not to be messed with as he divides the world blatantly in friends and foes. He emphasizes an "America First" approach and uses Reagan's election slogan "Make America Great Again".

Trump stands for American exceptionalism the same way Obama, Schwarzenegger, or Reagan did: Obama as an African American kid growing up without a father, Schwarzenegger as an immigrant from Austria becoming California's governor, Reagan as an actor turned politician and Trump as a businessman without political experience. Trump symbolizes America and its values in his pursuit of getting ever richer and more powerful; he also symbolizes strong puritan (hard work and no alcohol) and family values.

At a time of politicians like a soft-spoken, Barack Obama, a Hillary Clinton and a "do-nothing" Congress is represented by Elizabeth Warren, Mitch McConnell and Paul Ryan somebody like a Donald Trump already stands out in terms of perception as a rough and authentic working-class hero. Donald Trump sees himself as the messenger and has taken to Twitter to sell his message.

His story is that politicians in Washington D.C. are clueless, incompetent or have been bought and now they have sold out the American public to foreign governments, special interest groups or they don't know any better. In any case Americans are doomed unless they elect a successful businessman who knows how to get things done and bring him in as a game changer powered by the will of the people to break up the stalemate in Washington and look after what Americans really want. No more intermediaries just the new leader of the people to give the American people what they want and deserve.

Donald Trump has a natural intuition for how to connect with everyday Americans and is staying away from social-conservative topics. Many voters see in him a "lion" who can change the stalemate in Washington, DC, as there is a broad consensus across the parties (see Bernie Sanders) that the political system is rigged and only rich people can make themselves heard, by buying themselves influence and the laws that help them to get even richer. He carefully nurtures his image as an outsider, a successful businessman who gets things done and wastes no time with political correctness and who is independent from lobbies.

From Michael D'Antonio in his book *Never Enough:*

Perhaps nothing in nature is more voracious than this man's hunger for wealth, fame, and power. And it is this force that has allowed him to endure considerable mockery and substantial setbacks in business and still come back for more. Indeed, after his humiliation at the correspondents' dinner in 2011, Trump nurtured an ambition to mount his own campaign for the American presidency— a real campaign and not another of his flirtations—and thereby claim the greatest accomplishment available to a person in the twenty-first century. (10)

There is, however, a vulnerability to Trump in private that the public often does not see; he comes across as genuinely wounded that he is not taken seriously. In one interview, he was upset that his fellow billionaires don't show him respect. "Murdoch has been very bad to me," he said. "Bloomberg has been quite bad to me. I thought he was a friend of mine; he's no friend of mine. He was nasty." Michael Bloomberg even gave a speech at the Democratic convention in favor of Hillary Clinton. (11)

As Michael D'Antonio wrote in his book *Never Enough*:

> In the winter of his life, Donald Trump remains fully committed to his pursuits, which include fighting, consuming, and marking the planet with his name. Any linguist or psychologist could write at length on Trump's conversational style. After the briefest reflection, he slams the door on introspection and turns immediately to consider other people and their failures. A mention of books leads him to discuss his own book and its sales and then the corresponding success of his TV show. Trump represents in so many ways our times. Yes, he can be boorish and obnoxious and is unnecessarily cruel. But considering the world as he found it, Trump should also be regarded as a genuinely successful man who triumphed in the winner-take-it-all game. He is a living example of the values of our time. Wealthy and universally recognized, he established himself in the public mind first as a developer, but went on to occupy two more prominent positions—game-show host and politician. (12)

His most important characteristic that sets him apart from other candidates and serves him well in his campaign against Hillary Clinton is his authenticity. His language, his use of media (he tweets by himself and retweets a lot, which sometimes brings him into trouble), the style of his rallies and speeches (no teleprompter), his style (red cap), and his spontaneity all contribute to this perception. His pundits interpret it as his having no impulse control or pathologically lying, but his followers see it as the key reason they like him and are unabatingly loyal to the point that negative news, ads, and attacks cannot hurt him.

Some of the moments on the campaign trail and in interviews are especially telling of this, such as when he conceded in an interview with Megyn Kelly ("Megyn Kelly Presents" on May 17 on FOX), after she had reached out to him after nine months of him boycotting her, "I'm a real person. I would not have done this. I don't say it as a positive about me, I say it as a negative." Or in the same interview, when he said, "I'm also a human and I'm fighting for survival." Or in his rallies, when he says, "There have been so many negative ads against me. Some of them are true but 95% of them are wrong." Besides his narcissism, he manages to come across as witty and tongue in cheek in moments like those. (13)

The Brand

With his real estate holdings, his books, his presence in the tabloids, and most of all his reality TV show "The Apprentice," Donald Trump has built a brand that stands for wealth, opulence, and success. The fact that some of his enterprises have declared bankruptcy does not hurt that image but strengthens his image as someone who can take punches and get up off the mat again while others without his fortitude and ingenuity would have crumbled.

Donald Trump has built an impressive business, which currently employs over 22,500 people and is worth $4–$10 billion, depending on the source. It's an American brand. The Trump name adorns luxury condominiums, hotels, and golf courses around the world; it has sold a TV show, millions of books, a line of cologne, and even, briefly, an airline. He has succeeded in very different industries (construction, entertainment, consumer products, publishing) and on a global scale.

> *"The Apprentice"* added "TV star" to Trump's long resume and confirmed, at last, that he was as much entertainer as businessman. The program showed how he was about popular culture and how he could materialize the value of celebrity. It also made him and his brand known to a new generation of Americans. Trump came to represent wealth mixed with vulgarity and a hedonism that was refreshingly honest. Trump's image was often used in the news media to signal that a report was about money, wealth, or luxury. The word Trump

became synonymous with both unabashed success and unseemly self-promotion. To say that someone was "the Donald Trump" of this or that, which happened often, was either a high compliment or a put-down. By 2014, Trump was a walking Rorschach test. In him one could see extreme examples of ambition, obsession, aggression, and insecurity. He also exhibited creativity, strength, and candor. Trump's peers in business reported that he was honorable and consistent, although he has sometimes been criticized for being slow to pay his bills. With a few exceptions, employees described him as demanding but generous with pay and benefits. They describe him as quick-witted, funny, and charming. Words flow from him like water from a spigot, even if some of the anecdotes he continues to tell have been repeated for decades. Trump also gave the lie to the notion that he doesn't care what people think of him. His many feuds and conflicts suggest he worries a great deal about how he is perceived and whether he is judged to be a winner or a loser, handsome or hideous, strong or weak. While he says that he is driven by the thrill of competition, his bully-boy quality is a sign that something else has pushed him to overwhelm his opponents, run up the score, and dismiss those who speak against him." (Excerpted from Michael D'Antonio's book, *Never Enough*, 2015)

There is however also another side to the Trump brand and it is represented by his daughter, Ivanka Trump. Just as consistently as her father makes inflammatory statements his daughter offers her 2 million Twitter followers tips on such noncontroversial topics as sleeping better and dressing chic for #WomenWhoWork. Ivanka shies from the TV news shows her father thrives on, but she is increasingly appearing in *Vogue*, *Elle Decor*, and other glossy magazines aimed primarily at women. She would never offer an off-the-cuff, outrageous statement. She is clearly focusing on her family and business and therefore trying to protect the Trump brand as a business. (14)

The Media Hype

Donald Trump knows how to use and play with the media; he is a master at that. No other candidate for the presidency before him has managed to get so much free media, close to $2 billion between June 2015 and April 2016. (15)

The common belief in the US and around the world that US presidential elections are "all about who can raise more money from big corporate interests" does not apply in the 2016 election. While Hillary Clinton and Jeb Bush, as well as later Clinton, Marco Rubio, and Ted Cruz, were funded mainly by large donations it did not make the crucial difference in primary success. Bush reached a new record in political fundraising by having raised $115 million as early as June 30, 2015, and Cruz and Rubio had also raised between $40 million and $63 million at that time. Donald Trump arrived without any funds and even by the end of January 2016 had spent hardly any money. Donald Trump succeeded, and Bush was done as early as of end of January, despite having raised a lot of money. No wonder he is still very angry at Donald Trump and cannot understand how it all happened.

On the Democratic side, Hillary Clinton had raised close to $200 million by the end of January 2016, mainly from Super PACs and large donors (over 80% of total), but Bernie Sanders was thriving politically and soared in terms of campaign funding based on small donations at an average of $27 per donation despite being widely regarded as an underdog and hardly any chances to claim the nomination.

Some of his controversial statements break the record for news stories; for example, his idea of a temporary ban on Muslims entering the United States broke over twenty-five thousand articles on Google in a week. In terms of bought versus earned (free) media, Jeb Bush bought $82 million in ads before the South Carolina primary and earned $214 million; Trump bought $10 million and earned close to $1.9 billion. (15)

Instead of what historically would have been a couple million, twenty-four million viewers saw the first Republican debate. CNN and Fox

News saw their highest ratings in history and thrived on the Donald Trump phenomenon. The main attraction and the reason for so many people tuning in was clearly Trump; the debate was a mix of politics and reality TV and entertainment news or a *Survivor* show. It even got higher ratings than the NBA finals, the World Series, and some NFL games.

> No wonder the CEO of CBS declared, "It may not be good for America but it's damn good for business," referring to the high ratings that Donald Trump coverage has brought. (16)

In his interview in front of journalism students of the University of Chicago asked about the media and Donald Trump, Jon Stewart said,

> "The media has subsumed to the powerful. Fox News understood that you have to be perpetuating your point of view and relentless in enforcing your propaganda. Trump is relentless, ubiquitous. You want 24-hour networks to be incentivized for clarity but they are incentivized for conflict. Voices that are amplified are the most extreme and conflict provoking. This is the first season of *Survivor* all over again, reality TV. First he is an enormous dick and then when it comes to final counsel he reveals that his grandmother died and he is really a nice guy." (17)

WEAK OPPONENTS

Jeb Bush was a weak establishment front runner, and Marco Rubio or Scott Walker quickly raised doubts about their preparedness. Ted Cruz was strongly opposed by party elites and had so little appeal to voters who didn't consider themselves very conservative that he couldn't win the nomination.

Jeb Bush got derailed early as he failed to position himself on any topic and was therefore positioned by Donald Trump for being weak on

illegal immigration and as "low energy," a characterization that is equal
to weak leadership. Marco Rubio had some strong moments early on
but showed immaturity and seemed robotic in the debate before New
Hampshire, where Governor Chris Christie attacked him vigorously.
Rubio lost most of his positive aura when, in a desperate last-minute effort, he suddenly began very personal attacks on Trump that were totally
uncharacteristic for him. Ted Cruz is a very good speaker and played
well his role as a Washington outsider, despite being a senator there;
however, although he tried hard to come across as the Ronald Reagan of
this election cycle, he never really appealed to a broader electorate than
pure conservatives.

There was no charismatic politician with a strong track record or no
real rival businessperson to compete with Trump besides Carly Fiorina,
who did not have a solid record to compete upon. If there had been a rich,
eloquent, and highly successful businessperson competing, maybe even
one with political and/or media experience, such as Michael Bloomberg or
Mark Cuban, it could have been far more difficult for Donald Trump to
win. Mark Cuban wrote about this election,

*"It may not seem like it sometimes, but this country does want exciting
new ideas. We want to know there is a positive direction for us."* He further
wrote, *"The future of this country can't just be about free stuff, raising taxes on
the rich or cutting taxes for everyone, keeping people out and undoing what is
already done. There are new ideas in this world that matter. It would be nice
to get one from a Presidential candidate."* (18)

Donald Trump's opponents had no shortage of ammunition. By
one calculation, 76% of his political statements last year were un-
true. In a normal year, his Republican critics would have stopped
him. Why did they fail? His unusual talents are part of the answer. Charismatic, tactically astute, charming at times, and ruthless, Trump is a far more formidable politician than almost anyone
had suspected. His outrages have kept print- and broadcast-media

attention focused on him; with over 23 million followers on Twitter, Facebook and Instagram, he rules on social media too. (19)

Hillary Clinton as the Democratic Nominee

No matter how tight the primary became for Hillary Rodham Clinton, the Republican primary candidates knew from the beginning who they would face in the general election, and so did the Republican primary voters. Therefore, part of the Republican primary election calculus was the question who could best beat her. Most political analysts early on gave Donald Trump a much better chance at defeating Clinton than they gave Ted Cruz or other, more traditional candidates, independent of any changing polls. Voters realized that Donald Trump had the most potential among Independents and Reagan Democrats.

Clinton is unbeatable on her political experience, especially when it comes to foreign policy. She is also very strong when it comes to the economy based on her husband's record in his time as president, when he oversaw rapid employment growth, a tripling of the stock market, and a budget that produced a surplus in his second term. However, she seemed vulnerable on her campaign trail as she was not seen as igniting a passion in or a strong connection with voters. In addition, it was unclear to people what strong convictions she had as many saw her as opportunistic, unauthentic and corrupt.

Most reporters were counting on a general election battle between Hillary Clinton and Jeb Bush before Donald Trump entered the race. Those two candidates were seen as having the best fundraising network and the strongest political dynasties behind them. However, when Jeb Bush could not convince voters why they should support him despite having a $100 million war chest, other candidates came under consideration. Ted Cruz was seen as too conservative to get the majority of independent voters in the general election, Marco Rubio as too immature to win in a fight with Clinton, and Ted Kasich as not charismatic enough and too nice to stand in a fight against Clinton.

Donald Trump brought some unique qualities to the general election fight. He was seen as a hard fighter, a real street-fighter type who would hit the Clintons hard on anything, from Bill's extramarital affairs to Hillary's being bought by special interests or her decision in favor of the Iraq War or her judgment in the e-mail scandal. His background as a successful businessperson was seen as an asset in the general election. He also knew how to use the media formats of today, from Twitter to the cable networks and talk shows. Trump enforced that image by mentioning frequently that Romney had lost the election four years ago because he wasn't on TV enough the two weeks before the election. Above all, Trump was seen as THE master salesperson and as authentic, which ran counter to people's perception of Hillary as smart but also very slick and fabricated.

Especially with Hillary Clinton having been the secretary of state during Obama's first term, Donald Trump could focus on his differences with Obama and therefore Clinton regarding their failures in foreign policy and how he would not be "stupid" or be "toyed with," by applying an "America First" approach.

President Obama can be seen as the first "international president" in terms of wanting to make America more like the world rather than bringing American values to the world. In many ways, the desire for a populist/nationalist might be a reaction to his foreign policy, especially in the second term. The Nobel Peace Prize winner was known to be less willing than other presidents to leverage US military might, and he often left foreign policy options off the table in favor of negotiations, peace accords, and international unity. Here are some examples:

*   Stepping back from consequences for Syria after they violated the Red Line (gassing their own people)
*   Constant trouble with Russia, such as Putin outmaneuvering Obama in Syria or buzzing US boats and planes frequently or intimidating diplomats

* China getting ever cockier in taking over the South China Sea, limiting access to other nations and refusing to allow a US Navy ship to dock on the mainland in April 2016
* Relinquishing the last American control over the Internet. The Commerce Department confirmed it would cede oversight over the obscure but powerful Internet Corporation for Assigned Names and Numbers (ICANN) against vocal critics in Congress and in the tech community
* Iran taking soldiers hostage and showing videos on national TV where they were crying and begging for their lives, despite a recently signed nuclear deal, billions paid by the US government
* Snubbing Israel and being in favor of lifting sanctions on Iran
* No real breakthrough success against ISIS in Iraq, Syria, or Libya

The Republican Primary Modus

The Republican modus, although antiquated and undemocratic in some states, is still more open to outsiders than the Democratic one. In the Democratic primaries, a significant number of so-called superdelegates basically decide the election. As all states reward their delegates in a proportional manner in the Democratic primaries, those 715 superdelegates yield much power and are in most cases the deciding factor. Most of them decide who they support even before the primary yielding advantage to the party establishment candidate. As most of them make up their minds on who to support before voting starts they are yielding an unfair advantage to the party establishment candidate. So even if Sanders had won a victory in the primaries, he would have been denied the nomination. The fact that the Republican Party has no comparable superdelegates system and the primary calendar was much tighter this year, with more decisive primaries early on, helped Donald Trump.

Trump's Marketing Strategy

The Start

Before Donald Trump gave his announcement speech on June 16, 2015, at Trump Tower, he told his oldest son, Donald Trump Jr., "Now we will find out who our friends really are." In his forty-minute speech, he touched on many topics, but two stuck especially: Trump's wanting to become president to make America win again and his comment about Mexico sending the United States its worst people. (20)

It was a calculated move to get the conversation going and claim theme leadership without the other candidates being able to respond adequately. Immigration has always been a hot-button topic, but while no solution has been achieved politically, it is still one of the most important topics for Republican primary voters. While the statement immediately hurt Donald Trump and his company business-wise (Macy's, NBC, and many other companies instantly started boycotting him), it created high media coverage and a loyal fan base and put everybody else on the defense. It was a polarizing statement that antagonized many Hispanics but also initiated the start of an unconventional political campaign. Of course it came with a steep price as the media reported broadly that he would denigrate all Mexican immigrants, leaving out the distinction between legal and illegal immigrants.

Donald Trump was up against sixteen other Republican candidates, most of them experienced politicians. The last time somebody without any prior political experience became the nominee of a major political party was in 1940, when Wendell Willkie challenged FDR. But Trump has a lot of experience in business and also with politicians from being in the real estate business. In the real estate and construction industry, it is so important to know how to charm and win over politicians. City politics are a big influencing factor, and the feuds between Trump and the then mayor of New York City Ed Koch are proof of that. The Trump variation on the basic real estate recipe often includes a dollop of political grease and a little show business spice, for the sake of publicity. The precise mixture depends on the location, the competition, and the level of public interest. Good press can influence those who might buy or rent at a certain location. (21)

THE STRATEGY

Everyone who wants to really understand the core of the Trump phenomenon needs to understand marketing. That's where the real-life business experience of Donald Trump became the determining factor in this primary season. He knows how to leverage Social media and traditional media to maximize buzz and free coverage for the strongest and most direct connection with voters. He built his campaign around his authenticity and transparency in stark contrast to all the traditional politicians and his image, language, style, events, and media usage serve as the perfect reasons to believe.

It seemed many times that his contenders in the Republican field were still playing by the old rules while he was already playing by a new set of rules. That's how different this game was. Donald Trump played and used the media instead of them using him, and he led during the whole campaign by issuing new statements whenever he needed more buzz and wanted to force his topics onto the other candidates, therefore defining them instead of letting them define themselves. Today everybody remembers what Trump said about Jeb Bush, but nobody remembers what Jeb Bush really stood for.

As with new product introductions in business, Donald Trump positioned himself very narrowly at first, created high passion among a fan base, and generated attention and interest. He monitored attention and media buzz, and whenever they dropped, he launched a new targeted statement that reinvigorated and grew the base again, put him on top of chatter, and forced the competition to react. This way he could stay on top and force his game on the competition.

The prerequisite for this to work was to stay on top of the polls and to build a self-reinforcing marketing machine. Trump could quote polls that showed how much people liked what he was saying. The high poll numbers supported the perception of ever more voters that no matter how outrageous his behavior there had to be something to it as so many people agreed with him. This way he could position himself as the people's advocate and characterize anyone opposing him as bought or biased or just weak or too political correct.

He created a self-enforcing cycle of news, attention, curiosity, and interest, and to be competitive in the game of ratings and advertising money, the media was forced to report news about him as it broke, because he was always on top of the polls. The media coverage led to more people seeing his message and ways of delivering it. Meanwhile his competitors had to react to his themes or statements and were not able to position themselves but were positioned by him. He used poll results to ask for more coverage and special treatment and as a platform to show prospective voters how they could be "on the Trump train" and become winners by just banking on that trend.

For Donald Trump, it was all about marketing, as he also highlights in his book *Crippled America*:

> "*Sometimes I make outrageous comments and give them what they want—viewers and readers—in order to make a point. I'm a businessman with a brand to sell…The cost of a full-page ad in the New York Times can be more than $100,000. But when they write a story about one of my deals, it doesn't cost me a cent, and I get more important publicity. I have a mutually profitable two-way relationship with the media—we give each other what we need. And now I'm using that relationship to talk about the future of America.*" (22)

Donald Trump's Powerful Narrative and Storyline

* This is how I would describe the narrative Trump wants to bring across. "Us the people vs. them—them being the politician establishment, the media, the special interests. No wonder they oppose

me as they like the rigged political game where they can wield influence, but I'm not playing their game as I'm in it for you."

- Real change can only come from an outsider and successful businessman like him. Only he can solve the political mess in Washington, DC.
- Simple three-part narrative to attract the despondent demographic: America is losing; Donald Trump is a winner; and if Trump becomes president, America will become a winner, too.

During the primaries, Trump seemed to have discovered a strange formula. More often than not, when Trump said something particularly divisive, his poll numbers went up. This can be best explained by his unique appeal as a political outsider and the perception that he is an authentic candidate. It has also helped him to build a reputation as a doer that has no time to waste for political correctness, as he has claimed.

Product Adoption Life Cycle

Donald Trump has said, *"I'm the creator of my own comic book, and I love living in it."* (23) Trump introduced his political brand as a business would introduce a new product. First it is presented to a very engaged market segment with strong performance messages to build a fervent fan base. Once that is accomplished and the brand is loaded and stands for something, it is ready to expand to other areas, usage occasions, or in Trump's case, other segments of the population and other areas of policy. While Trump has never changed the core of his brand promise, he successfully transcended his messaging and expanded his base during the course of the primaries. From a mere 3%–5% of the country backing him, he has arrived at 40-47% of the electorate, according to the latest polls. It is the classical product-innovation lifecycle, from appealing to the innovators and early adopters of a new idea first and later to the early and late majority.

OBJECTIVE
Success, winning for Americans.

VISION
Make America Great Again; Make America Safe Again (after Orlando attack); "America First" Foreign Policy; Law and Order (after attacks on police)

STRATEGY

* Building a border wall against illegal immigration, destroying ISIS, banning immigrants that want Sharia law
* Commonsense politics that only an independent businessperson can pursue
* Less regulation, waste and lower taxes
* Solving the Washington, DC mess
* No corruption like the ties between the Clinton Foundation and the State Department
* Better trade deals for American workers and manufacturing sector
* "America First" foreign policy that is based on "peace through strength"
* Law and Order

POSITIONING
Only a winning businessperson can make America a winner again and, as an outsider, bring commonsense and straight talk to Washington, DC. Only he can solve the issues you care most about, because he will be your champion fighting for you in a tough, relentless and authentic way, independent from lobbyists.

RTB (REASON TO BELIEVE)

* Highly successful (rich) businessman (look at his brand, buildings, ratings, books, wealth)
* Great private life and family ("look at his children")
* Self-funded campaign
* Authenticity
  * No politically correct talk, "says it like it is"
  * His language, body language, use of words—no use of teleprompters
  * His campaign events in stadiums, hangars, fairgrounds
  * "Disintermediation" (no pollsters, no consultants, direct connection with voters via Twitter)
  * Spontaneity (entertaining as you never know what to expect at the peril that he might say something outrageous)
* Number one in polls, big audience at rallies

I compiled the main reasons that Republican voters gave in different polls as to why they were supporting him (as you can see, issues and style reasons are mixed in here):

* His stance on immigration (the wall, against illegal immigration, against taking Syrian refugees as ISIS has claimed they will use them to get terrorists into the US, ban on immigrants that want Sharia law, safe zones in Syria vs. bringing them here)
* His business acumen, winning image
* Bringing jobs back as he is the only Republican candidate ever to go against disadvantageous trade deals
* Lower taxes, less regulation
* Support of the Second Amendment
* Independence, self-funded

- Tell-it-like-it-is style, authenticity, no political correctness, against the Washington DC establishment
- Taking care of veterans and strengthening the US military
- Toughness—he takes no crap from nobody, assertive, and decisive
- "America First" foreign policy
- Destroy ISIS, take the oil
- Law and Order candidate, supporting police

Donald Trump knew exactly how to position himself and intuitively segmented the electorate. It was and still is a balancing act and a risky strategy. Some of his more extreme statements fulfilled the role of galvanizing a loyal base of the Republican electorate (approximately 35% of primary voters, or 3-4% of Americans) and guaranteed an early lead at the polls and record-breaking free media coverage, but now they are being held against him by Hillary Clinton.

On His Changing Views on Many Topics

Donald Trump said at the primary debate in Michigan on March 3, "*I have never known a successful person that wasn't flexible.*" He is automatically more trusted by voters despite his changing views as he is given the outsider and nonpolitician treatment. It seems that Trump is held to an entirely different standard based on his role. Voters also didn't care that he wasn't yet so versed on many topics, as they acknowledged that as a nonpolitician he still had to learn a lot and he seemed to have covered their hot-button issues.

On His Authenticity

Mark Cuban, the notorious owner of the Dallas Mavericks and TV star of the show *Shark Tank*, writing on his social media platform Cyber Dust on July 28, 2015, succinctly and effectively explained the Trumpian appeal: "*I don't care what his actual positions are. I don't care if he says the wrong thing. He says what's on his mind. He gives honest answers rather than prepared answers. This is more important than anything any candidate has done in years."* (24)

On Political Correctness

Other candidates work hard to relate their lives to the struggles of ordinary voters. Trump does the opposite, encouraging Americans to savor vicariously his billionaire's privilege of saying whatever he damn well pleases. "I love Donald Trump because he's so totally politically incorrect. He's gone after every group," said Greg Casady at a Trump rally (reported by Time magazine on Jan. 7, 2016 in the article "The art of the steal"). "He is spending his own bucks—therefore he doesn't have to play the politically correct game. He says what we wish we could say but we can't afford to anymore."

On Disintermediation

In terms of his media strategy, Trump seems to be already ahead of many other Republicans. Disintermediation has reached presidential politics, where candidates can cut out the middleman, or the media, thanks to social media. Donald Trump is history's most disintermediated presidential front runner. He has sidestepped the traditional middlemen—party, press, and pollsters—to sell his candidacy directly to voters, building on a relationship he has nurtured with the public from project to project across decades. He even writes, tweets and retweets mostly by himself not like others who have a whole Twitter team engaged. He has grown his Twitter audience to over 10 million and his total social media following to over 23 million followers. In today's media world, voters are more trusting of news coming from social media sites such as Facebook and Twitter, especially if it is forwarded or liked by their friends and peers. There is a mantra nowadays especially with digital natives: "If the information is important, it will find me." Marketing is at the core of the brand empire and runs in the veins of the Trump family. The way he branded and repositioned his competitors was masterfully done, and he now is trying to do the same with Elizabeth Warren (she suddenly started attacking Donald Trump on Twitter) and Hillary Clinton. Here are the names that he called his competitors frequently:

* "Lyin'" Ted
* "Low-Energy" Jeb Bush
* "Little" Marco
* "Goofy" Elizabeth Warren
* "Crooked", "Lying" Hillary

The name "Crooked Hillary" is especially well-crafted as it uses a word popular among older women, which is exactly the demographic that Clinton performs best with right now. It seems that Clinton is slowly getting the message that she is up against a marketing genius and one of the best salespeople in the world. She decided to change her campaign slogan on May 22 from "Fighting for Us" to "Stronger Together" to make a point about Donald Trump being divisive. However, it is never a good sign in marketing if you are changing a slogan in response to a competitor.

Donald Trump doesn't need consultants for his marketing strategy or a big team of spin doctors as Hillary Clinton does, as he is the mastermind behind his marketing campaign and sales pitches. According to people who know him well, such as Barbara Corcoran (*Shark Tank*), he is unbeatable as a salesman, with nearly magical appeal. Trump's political messaging has been like a rich uncle telling voters what is happening and communicating in self-confident, clear, rough language.

Looking deeper into the most important marketing principals, you can see how he and his campaign have applied them in this political campaign (the following laws are based on *The 22 Immutable Laws of Marketing* and

The 22 Immutable Laws of Branding from Jack Trout and Al and Laura Ries):

Law 1 (Law of Leadership)
Donald Trump was the first candidate to claim he would stop illegal immigration with a very believable reason to believe (the wall). He was the first to be self-funded and the first on the Republican side to call NAFTA, TTIP, and other trade deals bad for American workers. He was also the first to criticize the Iraq War, the first to ask for a ban on immigration from people supporting Sharia law and the first to call on the United States to take the oil from ISIS.

Law 2 (Law of Category)
Donald Trump created for himself the category of outsider businessman without political correctness for immigration control, better deals on trade, and an "America First" policy.

Law 3 (Law of Mind)
Clearly Trump wanted to be first in mind all along. He dominated the buzz and the polls, and whenever someone came close, he either attacked them in the most brutal and effective way possible, or he put out a new statement that created a fresh news cycle he could be the epicenter of.

Law 4 (Law of Perception)
Reality doesn't exist, what we call reality is just a perception of reality that we create in our minds. Donald Trump is a master of this, creating the perception of this narrative in my opinion: "American workers are losing because incompetent politicians do bad deals with other countries and don't

secure our borders. They are either incompetent or do the wrong thing because they have been bought. Trump is a winner and can come in as an independent outsider to fix it all: secure the border, negotiate better trade deals, and replace incompetent politicians with experts from the business world. This way America wins, and American workers will win as well."

Law 5 (Law of Focus)
Donald Trump is focused. He talks about only the same four or five topics constantly, repeats his messages, and always talks about winning. He wants to own the words "real" and "winner" in voters' minds.

Law 6 (Law of Exclusivity)
Nobody could take away the authenticity and the winner image from someone like Donald Trump, who has billions, has a beautiful family, lives in Trump Tower, and has his own 747 jumbo jet and perfume brand.

Law 7 (Law of the Ladder)
Donald Trump had to be number one in the polls as he entered the race and keep it there. That is why he spent so much time in debates and at rallies quoting his poll numbers and later his delegate wins. As much his way of keeping score in life is money, in politics it is polls, and he uses polls all the time to build even more momentum.

Law 15 (Law of Candor)
At first he violated this one as he would not admit making any mistakes. However in his best speech so far on Aug. 18 in Charlotte, NC he said that he regretted things he said, especially if they hurt people.

The 22 Immutable Laws of Branding
The 22 Immutable Laws of Branding by Al Ries and Laura Ries

The Law of Publicity
The birth of a brand is usually accomplished with publicity, not advertising. Nothing could be truer of Donald Trump's campaign. He invested only a mere $10 million in advertising and had a couple of ads at a time when his main competitors had each produced eighteen ads and spent between $30 million and $100 million in advertising. Trump's earned media value, however, was seven (!) times higher his next rival's and three times higher than Hillary Clinton's, despite much higher advertising spending on their parts.

The Law of the Category
Donald Trump has become the leading brand in the Republican franchise, so over time he can be expected to widen the reach of the Republican Party and create a much bigger category for it. Maybe going forward many of his voters will be labeled Trump Republicans. (25)

TRUMP'S SUPPORTERS
He started out with getting around 35% of the Republican primary vote, mainly from white men with a high school education. However, as the race progressed and the field dwindled down, he started winning majorities of over 50% and even over 60% and gained support from other groups, including college students and women. Evangelical Christians have been drawn to Donald Trump from early on despite his being thrice married and irreligious. Most likely his support there stems from his business record, family values, and strong stance on the military.

He has brought more voters to the Republican primaries than ever, 10 million more than in 2012. In total 30 million Republicans, 28 million Democrats, and 25% of all eligible voters participated in the primaries, which is the most ever.

Key Characteristics of Trump Voters in the Primaries

It's a myth that Trump owes his support only to disaffected blue-collar workers. On average, people earning under $50,000 make up 29% of the electorate in primary states with exit polls, and 32% of Trump's voting base. However, those earning over $100,000 account for 37% of the electorate and 34% of his base. According to the RAND Corporation, a better predictor of whether someone is a Trump supporter is the answer yes to the question "Do you feel voiceless?" And voters who agreed with the statement "People like me don't have any say about what the government does" were 86.5% more likely to prefer Trump. (26)

THE MOST EFFECTIVE CAMPAIGN

His campaign was started and led like a startup and a scrappy outsider campaign. It is an example in effectiveness and keeping it lean. It is a great example of how much more effectively he could run the American government than other politicians could.

Not more than four people helped him to start his campaign all the way to Super Tuesday: Corey Lewandowski, Dan Scavino, Michael Glassner and Hope Hicks. Paul Manafort only joined as of Mar. 28th, well after Super Tuesday. The last time Lewandowski ran a campaign was in 2002, when he managed a losing Senate reelection bid in New Hampshire. Hicks and Scavino spent zero time in politics before this. The entire Trump campaign employed about a dozen people. He had no pollsters, media coaches, or speech writers. He focus-grouped nothing. He bought a few ads, and when he did, he wrote them himself. He also writes his own tweets, his main vehicle for communicating with his supporters. And it was his idea to adopt Ronald Reagan's slogan "Make America Great Again!". "I'm the strategist", Trump told a reporter. (27)

Trump ran a bare-bones operation, especially when compared to Hillary Clinton's swanky eighty-thousand-square-foot headquarters in Brooklyn Heights. Thanks to the small team they can respond to events quickly; for example, when the pope suggested Trump might not be a Christian owing to his plan to build a wall along the border, the campaign struck back within minutes. "If and when the Vatican is attacked by ISIS, which as everyone knows is ISIS ultimate trophy, I can promise you that the pope would have only wished and prayed that Donald Trump would have been president," his statement said. By contrast, Clinton's tweets are vetted by layers of advisers; it's very controlled. (27)

Trump invented the idea of doing events at airports because it is cheaper than renting a ballroom and it saves time. Trump relies mostly on free Instagram spots produced by twenty-nine-year-old Justin McConney, the son of his comptroller. Trump is cheap, and proud of it. It's part of Trump's central argument: he will run the government like a business. (27)

Donald Trump applied the Silicon Valley approach for startups to his campaign. The idea is to arrive at a product over time that has evolved enough that people really like it. Think of the way he would cycle between demeaning nicknames for his opponents until one stuck. Of course, this is a perfect strategy for the social media and cable TV driven news cycle, then the premium is on novelty and outrageousness. Why should he spend that much when he has a system designed to dominate the news cycle? Start-ups find unusual routes to the market that allow them to do a lot more with stretched resources. (28)

THE COMPETITOR

Trump's competitors were clearly not as versed as he was in marketing, and so they let themselves get positioned by Trump. At the same time, their calculus was totally wrong as they focused their fire on each other instead of going after Trump. They totally underestimated his staying power on top of the polls and as the last survivor. Even up to Super Tuesday, they still celebrated their second-, third-, and even fourth-place finishes like victories. Donald Trump would say of himself that he is a perfect counter-puncher. He had a policy where he would wait until his opponent struck first, and only then he would react, but in such a strong way that this person would never repeat any strike.

He clearly did not fit in with the social-conservative candidates, but he did not care and basically made clear that the Republicans had the choice of picking a true conservative, and losing badly in the fall, or going with a populist who could fight against Hillary Clinton and build a strong connection to more Americans.

By breaking many political conventions, Trump put his opponents on the defensive, forcing them to respond to him and allowing him to set the tone for the primary contest. One of his moves was to deduce his critics' weak points and distill those into nicknames that stuck.

It's hard for competitors as they either risk being overshadowed by his media coverage or risk fierce personal attacks once they go after him. He has built an image of success and getting things done and strongly believes in himself. He cannot really be attacked on his positions as they are either popular with the electorate or voters vote for him based on his image as a successful entrepreneur and his authenticity.

The conservative senator Ted Cruz won his home state of Texas and the Iowa caucus, thanks to evangelicals. Christian religiosity seemed to be the strongest predictor of support for Cruz, by far. Cruz did much better with people that attend church regularly. They constantly charged that Trump was insufficiently conservative, but voters did not seem to care enough.

Donald Trump can come across as rude but also as very assertive. Trump justifies it like a boy in a fight, complaining that the other guy struck first. He is often right about this. Comedians, politicians, and others have picked on him for everything from his ego to his extravagant swoosh of bright blond hair. As a man who says he considers money to be a way to "keep score" in life, he has been especially bothered by those who suggested he isn't all that rich. (29)

Many voters, especially men, like to see a candidate that radiates strength and assertiveness, especially in times of political stalemate in Washington DC, and a perceived weakness of America in foreign affairs. Especially among the so-called Walmart voters, this made Trump the Porsche among the candidates. The debates and comedians mocking his behavior toward Jeb Bush further strengthened this perception. He is not somebody to be toyed or played with or somebody who can be ripped off by the other side. This is especially important in a conservative talk radio narrative, where the United States is seen as losing power globally and being outsmarted by Putin, Erdoğan, the Saudis, and other foreign leaders.

His competitive drive can be further explained by his upbringing and family background. In his family, male privilege was honored, but Donald's older brother (eight years older), Fred Trump Jr., was too softhearted for the behavior his father expected of him. As Donald watched his elder brother try to please their father, he felt sympathy for him. Trump men were supposed to be tough, even when dealing with each other, but when his father lashed out at Freddy, it was hard to watch. Freddy had been a kind and concerned sibling who lectured Donald on the dangers of smoking and drinking, two habits Freddy couldn't break. Learning from what he saw, Donald resolved to stand up to anyone who challenged him, including his father. Years later he would say, "I used to fight back all the time. My father was one tough son of a gun." However, he added, "My father respects me because I stood up to him." (30)

THE LANGUAGE OF A MASTER SALESMAN

HIS LANGUAGE

At the beginning of his political campaign for president, many reporters said that his speeches were incoherent and his words and grammar very simple. However, over the past several months, many linguists and researchers have discovered that his speech pattern, sentence structure, words, and even use of grammar fulfill a clear goal in effectively persuading his audience to a level where he has a clear competitive advantage and is even hypnotizing in a way. As a master salesman, Trump knows how to sell a feeling. By now his use of language has become one of his trademarks and even impact how some of us use it, whether words such as "huge" or phrases such as "Believe me."

One great example is his intuitively perfect answer to a question about his most controversial comment so far, the proposed temporary ban on Muslim immigration to America. Independent of the actual content, his answer shows exactly the secret sauce in his convincingness. To demonstrate how this works, YouTuber Evan Puschak recently dissected a 220-word, one-minute answer that Trump gave to Jimmy Kimmel when Kimmel asked about Trump's Muslim ban on Kimmel's talk show on December 17, 2015. (31) (Please also watch the full video on YouTube: https://www.youtube.com/watch?v=_aFo_BV-UzI&feature=youtu.be.)

Here is Kimmel's question:

"Isn't it un-American and wrong to discriminate people based on their religion?"

And here is Trump's answer:

But, Jimmy, the **problem** *— I mean, look, I'm for it. But look, we have people coming into our country that are looking to do* **tremendous <u>harm</u>**. *You look at the two — Look at Paris. Kook at what happened in Paris. I mean, these people, they did not come from Sweden,* **okay? Look at what happened in Paris. Look at what happened last week in California**, *with, you know, 14 people* **<u>dead</u>**. *Other people going to die, they're so* **badly <u>injured</u>**. *We have a real* **problem**. *There is a* **tremendous** *hatred out there. And what I wanna do is find out what it — you know, you can't solve a* **problem** *until you find out what's the* **<u>root cause</u>**. *And I wanna find out, what is the problem, what's going on. And, it's temporary. I've had so many people call me and say* **<u>thank you</u>**. *Now, if you remember, when I did that a week ago it was like* **<u>bedlam</u>**. *All of a sudden — and you watch last night, and you see people talking. They said, "Well, Trump has a* **<u>point</u>**. *We have to get down to the* **<u>problem</u>**." *The people that are friends of mine that called say, "Donald, you have done us a* **tremendous <u>service</u>**." *Because we do have a* **problem**.

Seventy-eight percent of the words in his answer have only one syllable, 17% have two, and only four words have three syllables. Nearly all of Trump's sentences terminate with a pointed, punchy word that contributes to his overall theme: "harm," "dead," "die," "injured," "problem," "bedlam." And instead of saying, "You can't solve a problem until you find out what the root cause is"—the natural way to structure that sentence—Trump brought the "is" forward to end on "root cause": "You can't solve a problem until you find out what's the root cause." He did the same thing a few seconds later as well: "I want to find out," he said, "what is the problem." Trump is so fond of this technique that even when his sentences don't end with punch lines, he simply follows them with a one- or two-word declaratory judgment—both in real life and on Twitter. One of his favorite endings on Twitter is "sad!" For example, Trump once tweeted, "Because of me, the Republican Party has taken in millions of new voters, a record. If they are not careful, they will all leave. Sad!"

The list of Trump's linguistic eccentricities goes on. He often speaks in the imperative mood, instructing his listeners to "look" at something ("Look at what happened in Paris. Look at what happened last week in California.") or commanding them to "believe" him, "trust" him or "mark [his] words" (in lieu of trying to convince them that what he's saying is, in fact, believable). "I will build a great, great wall on our southern border," Trump said in his announcement speech. "And I will have Mexico pay for that wall. Mark my words." Or "That's what politicians do: all talk, no action," he told AIPAC. "Believe me."

"The looseness of Trump's language just reinforces that there's a kind of perverse integrity to it," says Shesol, a speechwriter. "You might not like it. But he is who he is and he's happy to tell you about it." (32)

His recipe to connecting with his audience includes these ingredients:

* Using simple words and short sentences
* Ending every sentence strongly (powerful final words
* A lot of repetition (same favorite words)
* Implicating

This helps Donald Trump to emphasize the perception of being an outsider and a fixer, in contrast to politicians that sound sophisticated but do nothing. There is a new study out suggesting that Trump's emotionally charged language is exactly why his followers want him in the White House, as it makes him seem more presidential and trustworthy. It seems that voters appreciate it when a political candidate mirrors their emotions during times of economic hardships, as voters feel their own fears and uncertainties of the future are understood. David Clementson, at Ohio State University, said, "If you use low-intensity language in stable circumstances, you're more trustworthy. Researchers found that when we feel fearful or uncertain about the future, we are more receptive to intense, emotional language that mirrors our own feelings." Clinton's challenge is that there seems to be a double bind for female speakers as research has shown that people do not look favorably upon the use of this sort of emotionally charged language when it's coming from a woman. (33)

Previous research has found that the way "the Donald" speaks mirrors the average conversation—which makes supporters believe he is an honest outsider, Georgetown University linguist Jennifer Sclafani told *Daily Mail*. "His conversational style contributes to his overall image as a political outsider and as an 'authentic' candidate, which is an important quality to American voters." When he addresses the masses during debates and rallies, his sentences are fragmented and very simple. (33)

As more than 40% of Americans have only basic literacy skills, all candidates need to be able to talk to them. (34)

His Words

Linguists also looked at whether the language of candidates was more masculine or feminine. Hillary Clinton, no surprise, sounds the most feminine of the candidates on the campaign trail, commonly using phrases such as "incredibly grateful" and "open our hearts." More surprising, the second most feminine sounding speaker is Donald Trump, who often talks about "my beautiful family" and "lasting relationships." But unlike Clinton, Trump is just as likely to speak in overtly masculine language, especially favoring phrases such as "absolutely destroy" and often using words that tend to alienate women (and many men): "moron," "imbecile," and "loser." (35)

James Harbeck wrote an interesting analysis in *TheWeek* on how Trump uses repetition to create a stimulus-response effect and to make his simple ideas, labels, and attitudes stick. These are the main varieties of his repetitions:

1. Trump uses the same words and phrases incessantly and identically. These aren't just any words and phrases: they have strong emotional valuation. Win. Great. Huge. Sad. Weak. Lame. Lyin' Ted. Crooked Hillary. Goofy Elizabeth Warren.

2. Repeat a thing often enough, and it burrows into the mind and becomes a given. Trump's tweets often have a particular structure: "Wow, Lyin' Ted Cruz really went wacko today. Made all sorts of crazy charges. Can't function under pressure—not very presidential. Sad!" First he makes a declarative statement using insulting language. Then he expands on it. Then he caps it with a one-word evaluative summary. (36)

3. Trump uses the rule of three. He says the same thing three times, use the same structure three times, make sets of three. Sometimes he says nearly the same thing three times: "a strong, good, hard look," "building up our military, building up our strength, building up our borders." Sometimes he uses three related things: "waste, fraud, abuse," "China, Japan, Mexico." Sometimes he builds it up: "40, 50, 60," "People saw it. People liked it. People respected it." (36)

His Speeches and Rallies

Donald Trump gives forty-minute speeches without any teleprompter; he pounds the same messages with some current topics spread in. It is easy to digest and entertaining, with simple sentences with a clear good-versus-bad perspective, engaging to the audience, witty, and even tongue in cheek sometimes. He talks with his audience as with a friend, not about them. He repeats positive polls, all the wins, and mentions record audiences to make people feel good about themselves and their larger-than-life role. He likes big audiences at big venues such as hangars and fairgrounds or stadiums.

He loves to badmouth politicians, telling stories showing their incompetence and weaknesses (such as John Kerry participating in a bike race at age seventy-three and getting hurt while negotiating with the Iranians and basically losing the negotiations, in Trump's opinion, reminding voters about his core competence of negotiating). His narrative works for his audience, who is already convinced that all politicians are crooks, government is ineffective, and America's power in the world is declining. Without a teleprompter, he rants about others being low energy and sprinkles in rhetoric questions such as "I hit him hard, folks. Do we agree?" (about hitting Jeb Bush in the debates), using phrases and sentences such as "gravy train," "rigged system," "You wanna know the truth?" "Do we agree, folks?" and "I'll fix it fast, you won't even believe." He tells a story that resonates well and is easy digestible and never boring. He creates muscle memory with his audience and reaches them via social media, all the news channels, and debates.

Below are rules on how to speak like Donald Trump by Andrew Romano on *Yahoo*:

1. Interrupt yourself a lot. It's called digression and is a key characteristic of Trumpese.
2. Repeat yourself repeatedly.
3. Use intensifiers such as "very" often. Donald Trump uses a lot of superlatives; in Trumpese everything and everybody is either "the

best" or "the worst" without any in between. Other little words he likes to use are "so," "such," "really," and "totally"; he is obsessed with these.

4. Speak in slang. Donald Trump uses words and phrases such as "big league," and he often uses the word "guy" to describe world leaders and politicians.

5. Never use filler speech such as "uh" or "um" and is rarely silent. The question is whether he decided to speak that way or it developed over time. (37)

His Body Language

Based on Katrina Razavi's article in the Huffington Post, there are three body language strategies that Donald Trump uses to persuade, communicate, and get people on his side.

1. He uses obvious facial expressions. It doesn't take more than a quick YouTube search to reveal that Trump exaggerates his facial expressions to illustrate his emotions. In the debates, for example, whenever Jeb Bush was speaking, you couldn't help but focus your attention on the dumbfounded look on Trump's face. Once you watch Trump make that face, the same feelings of confusion are triggered thanks to mirror neurons.

2. He has a body language strategy. He uses his entire body. In all cases, notice how his posture is erect, his chin is level, and his chest is open. You can tell his chest is especially open and his shoulders are back when he's using both hands to gesture. If you watch Trump compared to the other candidates, you'll realize that he uses the most hand gestures compared to everyone else. Trump's hand gestures help solidify his story of being "high energy" and impactful. He uses hand gestures very effectively to keep the audience on pace with him.

3. He owns his appearance. The fake tan, the crazy hair, the pursed lips—Donald Trump clearly is who he is, and he owns it. Trump is being who he really is and is proud of it.

Trump is tormented on late-night talk shows, especially for his hair. But do you see Trump trying to change his hair? No, he will not change it. He's embracing what others see as a weakness, and he's accepting what he looks like. In a weird way, it's as if he's allowing himself to be vulnerable because he knows that vulnerability can increase likeability. Donald Trump is a unique communicator. He knows how to use body language to effectively convey his message and emotions and to influence other people's emotions. (38)

Where Obama's body language is pointed, specific, cool, humble, and less masculine, Donald Trump comes across as brash, masculine, direct, self-confident, decisive, loud, and energetic. His body posture and outfit enforce that further—a bombastic hairstyle, broad shoulders, and a confident look with open hand gestures.

Obama has a special hand gesture where he put his index finger against his thumb and points down whenever he says something important. It is called his "precision grip," whenever he is quite literally making a point. It makes Obama appear more pointed. Trump's most frequent gesture is the nog, an open-palm, double-hand downward motion. It makes him physically wider, which adds to the perception of his character. (39)

Mr. Teflon

One of the most interesting aspects of Trump's personality is the fact that negative news do not seem to impact him. No matter what he said or what the media reported about him it did not negatively impact his poll numbers. He said many divisive and outrageous things throughout the campaign but nothing really hurt him.

Even more astounding is the fact that the first time in US politics the most devastating weapon of pundits seems to be counterproductive: Negative ads. The method of launching huge ad campaigns to badmouth opponents and make voters afraid of the other candidate has a long, but not very proud, tradition in US politics. So far it has been one of the most effective campaign tools despite the fact that as collateral damage the reputation of politicians in general has tanked over the past decades.

Donald Trump was pressure tested during the Republican primaries as a number of anti-Trump PACs (PAC stands for political action committee, bundled money from special interests invested in advertising to support a cause or candidate) tried all kinds of attack ads. "He thinks we're fools," said an anti-Trump attack ad sponsored by the Conservative Solutions PAC, supporting Marco Rubio. "Trump picks on workers," said another, from the conservative nonprofit Club for Growth. Another nonprofit, the American Future Fund, which is backed by the industrialists David and Charles Koch, ran a series of profiles of Americans who say they were victims of fraud at Trump University. Those are only some of the attack ads that ran, for example, ahead of the North Carolina, Florida, and Ohio primaries. About sixty-thousand TV ads—roughly one-fifth of all ads aired during the Republican presidential primaries—were critical of Donald Trump, according to a Center for Public Integrity review of data from Kantar Media / CMAG. Despite this outpouring of hostility from his opponents, Trump swept the primaries with an absolute record number of votes in Republican primary history and became the Republican nominee. (40)

Polling data from states such as North Carolina, Florida and Wisconsin, show that anti-Trump ads did no damage to his support in those states, or nationally. There is even evidence from a research company that shows that those ads could actually have helped Donald Trump as it cemented his support among working class men. (41)

The key reasons why he seems to be the first candidate in US political history that negative ads have not hurt but actually helped:

* His voters feel a much deeper connection to him as he connects better than any candidate before him. The relationship feels more authentic for them due to his language, his direct connection via Twitter, his taking their voices seriously, and his lack of complicated or politically correct talk.
* His voters strongly believe that they already know him as an outsider businessman who has had a very colorful life with many life experiences he is not hiding (divorces, comments, business bankruptcies).
* His voters like him for being tough, rough, and a fighter. They do not hold him to the standard of other politicians or expect Mr. Nice Guy.
* Americans have become fed up with negative campaigning, and the effectiveness of that tool might have reached its saturation point.
* Americans trust Donald Trump more than they do the establishment politicians and clearly see through why the attacks are coming and from whom (the #NeverTrump movement). In addition Trump has already prepared his voters for those ads by discrediting the press and pundits.
* Donald Trump is a moving and unpredictable target, which makes him a dangerous target. In terms of policies and issues, he is hard to pin down owing to his ideological flexibility, and

in terms of unpredictability, everyone who attacks him risks a very effective and brutal counterpunch. His counterpunches so far have proven more effective than any attacks directed at him. Part of his counterpunch strength is his fervent social media fan base as well as his growing base of conservative news outlets supporting him.

Trump has always tried to establish a direct relationship with the public. For many, if not all, of these individuals, their networked relationships with Trump feel closer and more genuine than the images of the candidate they see filtered through middlemen. His followers feel that they already know him. And when outraged "middlemen"/news anchors hit on him, they only highlight their irrelevance to his followers. (42)

Donald Trump is experienced in crisis management. His celebrity life, in combination with his being a real estate developer in Manhattan, has hardened him and prepared him well for anything being thrown his way. The New York media and tabloid market is arguably the toughest in the world, and he has dealt with them for all his life.

THE NEW MEDIA GAME

Donald Trump incurred relatively low campaign costs—just $57 million through the end of April, of which he spent only $21 million on paid TV and radio commercials. That's about one-quarter of what Jeb Bush and his allies spent on TV.

The objective of media should be to bring clarity for voters and help them make choices about candidates in elections. However, the media is also driven by making money, and higher ratings mean higher advertising revenues, hence more financial success. The edgier a candidate is and the more conflict in the political arena, the higher the ratings, which lead to more coverage of that candidate, which leads to higher polls. It is a cycle that created a clear win-win for Donald Trump and media outlets this election season. Trump got enormous free media coverage, which helped him in the polls, and the media outlets sold more expensive advertising based on the high ratings that Trump delivered.

Biographer Michael D'Antonio says that there's a calculated "brilliance" to Trump's head-snapping utterances. *"He's told me that he is aware of how extreme the media is, and how you must be extreme to get attention,"* D'Antonio says. (43)

In all elections so far, the candidates tried hard to get as much coverage as possible, and the media picked and chose whom to feature when. In this election cycle, Donald Trump has turned around the whole process. As he knows about his value for media outlets to boost their ratings and improve their business results, he plays hard to get and lets them compete for his attention and participation. This has resulted in an unprecedented competition among news outlets to please Trump with better (more favorable) hosts and more frequent and better news slots than any other candidate would get. The media cannot get enough of him, and the ones more in need of a ratings bonanza have even adapted their news formats and shows around him. News anchors try to get him on air as much as possible to boost their ratings. He is very newsworthy. Instead of asking the media for attention, he lets people and the media respond to his ideas. He has completely reversed the political game by becoming the hot commodity that gets extra airtime that the media has to compete for.

Evan Puschak has created another very insightful video, in which he explains the interesting relationship Donald Trump has with the news media and vice versa (https://www.youtube.com/watch?v=9Tji1g0WrPw):

"There is a strong correlation between polling numbers and share of coverage, 0.96 correlation to be precise. It's a virtuous cycle for someone like Donald Trump: News coverage comes first, people research, name is more often mentioned to pollsters, poll numbers go up, candidate gets more coverage etc. A cycle that perpetuates itself until the candidate makes a mistake or a new face shows up and becomes more interesting. New fresh faces are the ones Trump attacked the most during the primaries. CNN is forced to cover Trump as he creates the news and delivers ratings. It's our nature as consumers to gravitate toward confirmation bias and sensationalism. Looking for objective and subject related information is a mental muscle we don't like to exercise. The news media, politicians and general public have all contributed to Donald Trump's rise." Evan Puschak (44)

When his unmediated celebrity converged with the rise of social media, Trump was ready to seize the moment, converting his TV fans into "friends" and "followers." (45)

CBS head Les Moonves said, "Man, who would have expected the ride we're all having right now...The money's rolling in and this is fun...I've never seen anything like this, and this is going to be a very good year for us. Sorry, it's a terrible thing to say. But, bring it on, Donald. Keep going. Donald's place in this election is a good thing." (46)

IS TRUMP OUR NEXT TV ANTIHERO?

Julian Zelizer, a CNN analyst adds an additional explanation to the Trump phenomenon in an interesting article for *politico* correlating the popularity of TV Anti-heros and Donald Trump's appeal. He describes how the audience has come to like the ambiguous antiheros and have come to prefer authentic personalities to perfectly virtuous protagonists, from *The Sopranos* to *Breaking Bad*, from *Homeland* to *24* to *House of Cards*. Donald Trump's candidacy seems like a product of this era. Some TV characters who are unlikable but emotionally relatable have long been the heart and soul of popular culture. Frank Underwood in *House of Cards* is an example of that ambiguity. We still want to see how he will find a way out of the latest jam, and want him to win. "In an era when so many institutions have become broken, from the economy to our politics, we find some kind of comfort in the person who shows the drive to get things done without letting that brokenness stand in his way." (47)

TWO SIMILAR REVOLUTIONS: SANDERS AND TRUMP

Donald Trump and Bernie Sanders have both tapped into the anger that is sweeping America this election season. They have both ignited the passions of Americans who feel increasingly disenfranchised from the politicians in Washington, DC, and the establishment of their parties.

SIMILARITIES BETWEEN SANDERS AND TRUMP

* Authenticity
* Enthusiasm, passion at events, rhetoric skills
* Easy explanations and solutions for the problems of the working class and middle class
    * Opposition to international trade deals such as NAFTA, TTIP
    * Ranting against lobbyists, special interests, and "bought" politicians
* Against the Iraq War
* Similar opinions on health care, trade, and campaign finance reform

Bernie Sanders and Donald Trump share many of the same oratorical tricks, from trumpeting their poll numbers to their pronunciation of the word "yuge" as they are both New Yorkers. At a CNN debate before the primary in New York, Sanders added two more similarities: he defended calling Hillary Clinton "unqualified" for the White House and argued the United States contributes too much to NATO. The commonalities on policy also extend to trade and labor issues, highlighting how the political "spectrum" is more of a circle.

Both reject the free trade agreements of the past two decades, including the pending Transatlantic Trade and Investment Partnership (TTIP) the largest trade deal in a generation. Both reject mechanisms to limit spending on Social Security and Medicare—and each supports his own version of health care for all. Both reject the use of super PACs to raise large political contributions and are convinced that politicians in Washington have sold out to powerful interests that contribute huge sums to campaigns.

The similarity between the two candidates was highlighted at a televised town hall in South Carolina on February 17, 2016. Mika Brzezinski, the MSNBC host, asked Trump to identify a candidate who fit the following description: "The candidate is considered a political outsider by all the pundits. He's tapping into the anger of the voters, delivers a populist message. He believes everyone in the country should have health care. This candidate," Brzezinski continued, "advocates for hedge fund managers to pay higher taxes. He's drawing thousands of people at his rallies and bringing in a lot of new voters to the political process, and he's not beholden to any super PAC. Who am I describing?" Trump replied, "You're describing Donald Trump." "Actually," Brzezinski declared, "I was describing Bernie Sanders."

Some union members are already dreaming of a common banner in a future election. "For decades I've believed, and voter research bears out, that there is a great majority of Americans who would flock to vote for a progressive who runs on a populist economic message and talks in simple terms," said Steve Rosenthal, president of the Organizing Group, a political consulting firm, and former political director of the AFL-CIO. Especially unions seem more and more divided between a new Democratic coalition that includes elitist and liberal views that favor globalization and strict environmentalism instead of the interests of their members. In 2016 several unions pledged allegiance to Donald Trump rather than Democrats.

Since 2006 many Democrats have won elections in campaigns against free trade, globalization, and any sort of moderate immigration policy. The difference between Donald Trump's and Bernie Sanders's populism is that Sanders focuses on economic populism and Trump economic nationalism. Nationalism begins from the same premise that working people are not doing so well. But instead of blaming the rich at home, it focuses its energy on the poor abroad. (48)

Here are three ways the candidates are similar according to Tamara Keith from *NPR*:

* Trump and Sanders both channel anger from people who feel the American dream is no longer within reach and the middle class is shrinking.
* They are both against super PACs.
* They believe American workers need fair trade policies. (49)

Both candidates have more in common than any of the other candidates. Their message is as follows: the system is rigged and the voters suffer from the inequality and crony capitalism in our system. Sanders blames Wall Street while Donald Trump blames incompetent leaders making bad deals with countries like China or Mexico. There is a strong protectionist sentiment in their comments. Both men's supporters are mostly white, mostly male, and express a strong disdain for the current political system. They are anti–political elite and believe that only an outsider can bring real change.

Differences between Sanders and Trump

* Personal attacks (Sanders does not engage in personal attacks)
* Political correctness (Sanders keeps with the Obama and Clinton tradition)

* Belief in capitalist system (Sanders claims that the billionaire class is the problem)
* Health care (Sanders wants free health care for all)
* Tax plans (Sanders wants higher taxes for everyone to pay for free college, health care, etc.)
* Immigration (Trump is against illegal immigration and taking refugees from Syria)
* Education (Sanders propagates free college and national standards)

A major Pew Research Center survey paints a vivid portrait of a divided and anxious American public. Forty-six percent believe that compared with fifty years ago, life in America today is worse for "people like [them]"; only 34% think that it is better. Fifty-four percent of whites say that things have gotten worse; only 17% of African Americans agree. Older Americans are twice as likely to perceive this decline as are young adults. Individuals with a bachelor's or more are inclined to see improvement; less educated Americans are not. 53% of Republicans believe that free trade agreements have been bad for the United States, compared with only 34% of Democrats. (50)

America has not yet had a nationalistic candidate with a socialist program, which is a very common phenomenon in Europe. What makes Trump interesting to Sanders voters is his authenticity, outsider approach, independence from lobbyists, and new ideas on trade and foreign policy. In conclusion Bernie Sanders voters have much more in common with Donald Trump than with Hillary Clinton when it comes to their demographics and the programs of the candidates. It will be interesting to see if Trump's pitch to those voters will resonate on Election Day. They could sway the general election.

CHAPTER 2

Clinton vs. Trump

———

THE BATTLE LINES

THIS GENERAL ELECTION WILL BE unique in many ways. It's the first time a woman has been nominated by a major party and only the second time in modern-day presidential politics that someone without prior military or political experience has been nominated by a major political party.

There's an argument to be made that both candidates actually deserve each other in terms of personal attacks, heated rhetoric, and how they treat the media. Hillary Clinton refuses to give press conferences and accepts only pre-negotiated questions while Trump criticizes the media any chance he has. All this has led to high disapproval numbers; they are the most disliked candidates ever in presidential history, according to polls, as a majority of Americans disapprove of both of them.

Who would have predicted in June 2015 that Donald Trump would become the Republican nominee with a comfortable margin after triumphing over sixteen other candidates? And who would have believed that Bernie Sanders, the self-declared socialist from Vermont who was not Democrat until a year ago, would become so hard to beat for Hillary Clinton, winning twenty-two states?

By now American, Democrats, and the press should have learned the lesson that Donald Trump is not someone to be underestimated. A more traditional candidate, such as Kasich or Cruz, would have been so much easier for Hillary Clinton to predict and beat. Nobody knows better than

Trump how to fight back and how to connect to voters and use the media his way. He is even hard to grasp and beat on policy because he is relatively flexible and unideological. On some issues like trade and foreign policy he is even left of Clinton. On the positive side, the candidates have more in common than candidates in the past. They agree on Social Security, investing in the infrastructure, Medicaid, Planned Parenthood, and many social topics that were divisive in the past, such as gay marriage. The biggest differences are in immigration, gun laws and foreign policy.

This election will be much less about specific policies and much more about persona. It will be about change and risk taking in picking a political novice or in going with someone very experienced who has been part of the Obama administration and in politics most of her life. There is no question that this will become the hardest-fought general election battle for president ever, after a very hard nomination fight in both parties that left the parties more fragmented than usual. At the end of the day, it will be revealed whether voters believe that Donald Trump or Hillary Clinton is the right person with the right ideas that America needs now, with independents and turnout being very important.

THE POLLS AND WHAT THEY TELL US

Donald Trump and Hillary Clinton are essentially in a dead heat since late July after Hillary Clinton had a strong lead in June. Based on the latest polls in August, Donald Trump seems even slightly ahead. Clinton wins handily when it comes to experience, personality and realistic policy proposals. Trump is more trusted when it comes to the economy, international trade and fighting terrorism. Trump also beats Clinton when it comes to taxes and "bringing needed change to Washington". Depending on the poll between 55-70% of Americans see Clinton as corrupt and only 30-40% of Americans trust her. Trump has built out a significant lead among Independents and it seems like his VP choice, Mike Pence, will help him to unify the party.

The question of whether voters are looking for a candidate with political experience or someone who comes from outside the political establishment remains a fault line of potential significance. Both candidates will focus in the last weeks of the campaign on the key battleground states and trying to discourage electability and therefore turnout for the other candidate. (1) Clinton is ahead by 14 points among women (50–36), yet Trump leads by a larger margin of 22 points among men (55–33). He also tops Clinton by 37 points (61–24) among whites without a college degree (working-class whites). (2)

Trump is winning 57% of white voters, while Clinton gets just 33%. For purposes of comparison, Obama in 2012 lost the white vote, 39–59. Among nonwhites, Clinton is at 69% while Trump is at 21%. Four years ago, Romney got 19% of the nonwhite vote. (1) Overall, Trump is preferred by 24 points among whites (55–31). He's even ahead by 9 points among white women (47–38). Clinton has a commanding 83-point lead among African Americans (90–7) and is up by 39 points among Hispanics (62–23). (2)

Based on a *Rasmussen* poll from July 24, 70% of Americans say that America is heading in the wrong direction and only 26% feel better off compared to before Obama took office, but still Obama's approval rating is at over 50%. It seems that voters like Obama's personality but not many see positive changes for themselves from his policies. This is the tough balance that Hillary Clinton has to strike between continuation and change. On the one side she tries to position herself as Obama's third term but at the same time her husband described her at the Democratic convention as the best change agent. (2)

KEY QUESTIONS THAT WILL DECIDE THE ELECTION
The key question that voters have to decide on this November is whether they want the continuation of the Obama administration and its policies or whether they want change. Do they prefer someone with vast political

experience stretching from the state politics, the Clinton administration, and Congress all the way to secretary of state, or an outsider businessman? Therefore, this election will be as much about Barack Obama and his legacy as it will be about Hillary Clinton. There are some predictable confrontations and battle lines this election season, but anything can happen, as the primary season has already shown.

Five Key Questions/Moments This Fall for Voters

* Continue with a third term of Obama or change?
* Who do you trust more on immigration, jobs and national security?
* Political experience or outsider businessman?
* How much will "pay for play" between Clinton Foundation and State Department hurt Hillary Clinton?
* The four debates (three presidential and one for VP)

The Ten Crucial Battle Lines – Hillary Clinton vs. Donald Trump

* Globalism vs. Americanism ("America First")
* Gun control vs. gun rights
* Black Lives Matter support or Law Enforcement advocacy
* Amnesty for illegal immigrants, no border wall, and sanctuary cities (Hillary Clinton) versus no amnesty for illegal immigrants, a border wall, and no more sanctuary cities (Kate Steinle case*)
* Same foreign policy as Obama but more hawkish versus "America First," which rewards key allies more and punishes foes harder. Tough sanctions against Russia and North Korea vs. negotiations with Russia and Kim Jong-un of North Korea
* How to best destroy ISIS? More Muslim immigration versus limiting immigration from countries supporting Muslim terrorism

* More trade deals like NAFTA—in other words, TTIP or not
* Obamacare expansion versus repeal of Obamacare
* Who will be better for jobs/economy and income growth?
* Budget deficit and tax reform

Ten Wild Card Topics

Besides those topics that will come up this election season as programmed, there are ten wild cards that could play a bigger or smaller role depending on current events or campaign strategies but could easily dominate the debate and decide the decision this fall.

* Another big terrorism attack in the US (similar to Orlando) or abroad (including subsequent debate on gun laws and if current strategy vs. ISIS is working)
* An economic slowdown (including subsequent debate on jobs and taxes)
* Violence against police officers
* E-mail affair (discussion on Clinton's judgment, her using BleachBit software to wipe her private server, the decision by the FBI to not indict Clinton despite her "extreme carelessness", future leaks as indicated by Assange – top 4 people of Democratic party have already resigned over leaks)
* "Pay for play" in the State Department in connection with the Clinton Foundation: rich foreign donors getting special access to Hillary Clinton in exchange for paying the Clinton Foundation or Bill Clinton for speeches like shown in the documentary *Clinton Cash* reporting how foreign governments and businesses made the Clintons rich by buying influence
* "Bill Clinton topics": the Epstein case, other Bill Clinton revelations
* Eventual government failures
* Any serious health issues being confirmed about Hillary Clinton

* Any revelations from Trump University trial, the release of his income tax returns (if released), or from Clinton's Goldman Sachs speeches

Kate Steinle case: In July 2015, Kate Steinle, thirty-two years old, took a stroll with her dad along a popular pier (Pier 14) along the San Francisco waterfront when she was shot in the back by illegal immigrant Juan Francisco Lopez-Sanchez without any previous interaction with him. She died in her father's arms. Lopez-Sanchez had stolen the weapon from a Bureau of Land Management ranger, who reported it stolen in June. Lopez-Sanchez was in the country illegally after being released from a San Francisco jail despite a request from federal immigration authorities that local officials keep him in custody for possible deportation. Lopez-Sanchez was previously deported five times to his native Mexico. San Francisco and thirty-one other cities in the United States have enacted so-called sanctuary policies of ignoring requests from Immigration and Customs Enforcement to hold inmates thought to be in the country illegally for deportation proceedings. The murder case and the broader immigration issue made waves in the presidential race. Donald Trump vowed to scrutinize existing sanctuary-city policies while Hillary Clinton indicated her support for the rules. (3)

A question that is always at the forefront of politics is the role of government, the size of government, and how it should be run. This election, the spotlight will be even more on this question as a businessman is running against an experienced politician. Symbolic of this is an interesting piece by Ed Rogers, who wrote in the *Washington Post* about this on May 25. He claims that long security lines at US airports are a problem for Hillary Clinton as it shows federal priorities and competence. He comments that the same people that rolled out the Obamacare website seem to be unable to figure out how to match the number of TSA security screeners with airport traffic. They should focus on topics like that rather than focusing on a school bathroom mandate for transgender students. (4)

The Battleground States

Let's start with what the electoral map looked like in 2012 (all of these maps are provided courtesy of 270towin.com): (5)

2012 Actual Electoral Map

Source: www.270towin.com

That map yielded Mitt Romney just 206 electoral votes—64 short of what he needed to win to be elected president. That 2012 map simply shows that Democrats have a big and nearly insurmountable advantage when it comes to national elections. It heavily favors Democrats at the moment. This election is Hillary Clinton's to lose.

Dan Balz, correspondent at the *Washington Post* pointed out in a terrific Electoral College analysis that Democrats have won eighteen states and the District of Columbia in each of the past six elections, going as far back as 1992. That means 242 electoral votes total. Clinton only needs to find another twenty-eight electoral votes to win the presidency in November. If she were to win Florida and its twenty-nine electoral votes, for example, plus those eighteen states and DC, she would be president. (6)

The general election between Trump and Clinton will be decided in the Midwest most likely plus Florida and North Carolina. Both candidates focus their resources currently on Pennsylvania, Ohio, Michigan as well as North Carolina and Florida. They invest the most money therein television ads, voter mobilization and hold the most rallies there.

On November 8, 2016, it will all come down to arithmetic as both candidates have to try to clobber together the right states to win 270 votes in the Electoral College. This is how the map looks right now. Clinton has 217 votes in the Electoral College and Trump 191 out of the total 538.

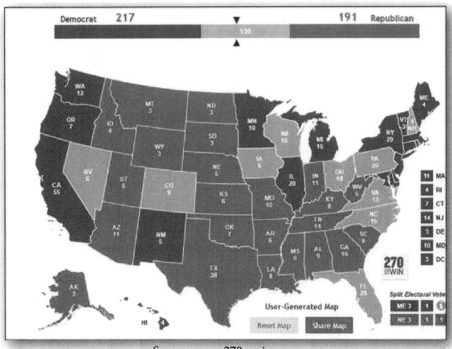

Source: www.270towin.com

It seems like there will be up to eleven battleground states (in descending order of electoral count): Florida, Pennsylvania, Ohio, Michigan, North Carolina, Virginia, Wisconsin, Colorado, Nevada, Iowa, and New Hampshire. The most important ones will be these five: Florida, Ohio, Pennsylvania, Michigan, and North Carolina.

Depending on how the trends develop, there would be consequences for this map:

- If Clinton lost some of her strong support expected among Hispanics, states such as Colorado, Florida, and Nevada would go for Trump. (7)
- If Clinton lost more of the union vote than expected over trade policies, states such as Ohio, Wisconsin, Pennsylvania and Michigan could turn red (Trump). The feedback from unions has been that many of their members are responding to Trump. (7)
- If Clinton lost more votes than Trump to other moderate parties or candidates such as the Green Party (the Al Gore scenario of 2000) or the Libertarian Party. (7)

Below you can see Clinton's road map to win. She already leads big in Colorado, Nevada, Wisconsin, and Virginia and slightly in Michigan. In this scenario she could become the next US president with a win in only one of these states: Pennsylvania, Ohio, North Carolina, and Florida.

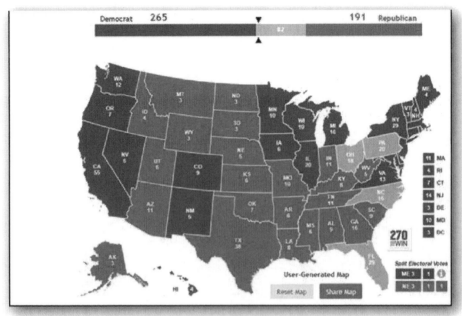

Source: www.270towin.com

For Trump, like any Republican, it is much harder to make the arithmetic work. He needs to win three out of the four most important battleground states besides Florida: Michigan, Ohio, Pennsylvania, and North Carolina. You can see that scenario below, where he wins all but Michigan:

Source: www.270towin.com

If Trump were to take only North Carolina and Ohio but not Pennsylvania and Michigan, he could only make it up by winning Nevada, Iowa, New Hampshire, and Virginia. If he were to lose Florida, which Democrats believe they have in their camp, he has to win not only Nevada, Iowa, Pennsylvania, and Ohio but also New Hampshire and Virginia. You can see that scenario below:

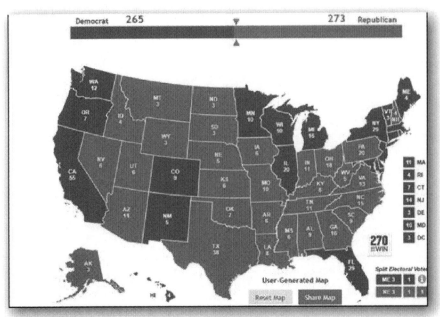

Source: www.270towin.com

There is also the case where it would come down to a 269–269 stand-off, which would be then decided by the House of Representatives electing the president, with each state getting only one vote, and the Senate electing the vice president, also with each state getting one vote. In this unlikely scenario, the president and vice president could even come from different parties.

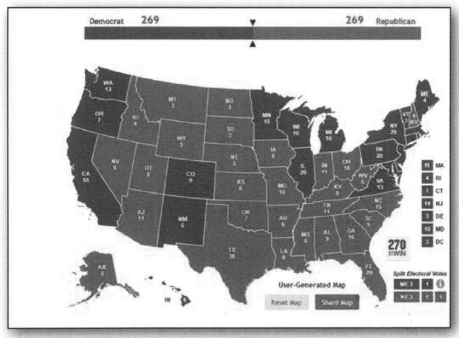

Source: www.270towin.com

The Debates

This election season points to a record audience for the TV debates, in the United States and around the world. This election is already being called the "Election of the Century," and the debates will have most likely a crucial impact on the result. There are three debates scheduled between Hillary Clinton and Donald Trump and one between the VP candidates, Mike Pence and Tim Kaine.

The Orlando attack in June

Obama and Clinton both used the attack to talk about gun control. However the real failure was in not preventing the attack as he was employed by security firms before and was interviewed by the FBI twice for terrorist ties. The idea there was improper follow-thru within the existing system seems to have occurred to no one in the media. The killer's father was a fervent Taliban backer who had talked to his wife and others about committing terror before. All these warnings signs were followed by trips to Saudi Arabia. Add to this his membership in a radical mosque and it's not clear that the current systems or administration is capable of putting any puzzle together that would have prevented this or any other home based attack.

Here is Trump's response, *"It's an assault on the ability of free people to live their lives, love who they want and express their identity. I refuse to allow America to become a place where gay people, Christian people, and Jewish people, are the targets of persecution and intimidation by radical Islamic preachers of hate and violence. This is not just a national security issue; it's a quality of life issue. We are importing radical Islamic terrorism into the West through a failed immigration system and through an intelligence community held back by the president. All terrorists committing acts in the US came through our dysfunctional immigration system. Immigration from Afghanistan has increased five-fold in just one year and 99% of people there support Sharia law. If we want to remain an open society we need to control our border. Hillary Clinton plans to admit many times more than the 100,000 coming from the Middle East every year; Hillary Clinton plans to grow the Syrian refugees' numbers by 500% without any plan to vet them or to prevent the radicalization of their children. This shooter was the child of an immigrant father who sup-ported the Taliban. Why would we admit people in who support violent hatred that leads to enslaved women and the murder of gays?"* He ended with committing to the ideal of America as a tolerant and open society but also a safe society that protects its borders at home and defeats ISIS overseas. (8)

Trump's response forced Clinton to use the term "radical Islam" for the first time. Obama used a press conference just days after the Orlando attack as a platform to promote gun control measures but even more to attack Donald Trump. It's unprecedented in American politics for a sitting US president to use a tragedy to launch emotional and sub-jective attacks on a candidate for president. Obama spoke in a highly contemptuous tone and would not want to declare radical Islam the principal problem. He did not see the point that an un-named enemy cannot be defeated. Ronald Reagan called the soviets the "evil empire" and declared the moral high ground setting the stage for eventual vic-tory. Obama showed an inability to understand and represent the mood of a nation at war.

Just days after Obama's statement John Brennan, CIA director, made clear that Obama's picture of the ISIS situation was way too rosy, Obama had said that his anti-terror strategy was "making significant progress". Brennan said, "ISIS remains a formidable, resilient and largely cohesive enemy." He further said," our efforts have not reduced the group's terror-ism capability and global reach. ISIS possesses a large cadre of Western fighters who could potentially serve as operatives and infiltrate refugee flows, smuggling routes and legitimate means of travel." (9) On June 21st, Marine Lt. Gen. Waldhauser said very bluntly that the US had obviously no strategy in Libya to fight ISIS and the current strategy of not bombing the group's affiliate there makes no sense. Waldhauser confirmed that ISIS represented an imminent threat to the US and that Africa was their next target. (10) That same day a former ISIS sex slave Nadia Murad, a Yazidi who escaped captivity urged Congress to do more to fight the terror group. She confirmed that without help the Middle East's Christians and Yazidis will be wiped out and detailed the torture thousands of women undergo due to ISIS and that they were planning more terror attacks like the one in Orlando. (11)

Obama continued to pretend everything was under control despite Orlando being the 7th ISIS attack on US soil since Obama took office, over 100 IS operatives have already been captured in the US and over 800 are being surveilled. Trump has shown resilience and authenticity on the issue. ISIS had declared war on the civilized world, whether Obama understood it or not. ISIS, as part of an overarching, Islamic Jihadism clearly resembles a modern-day Nazi party that can only be destroyed for continued freedom and democracy.

At the same time it is interesting to see how much Muslim immigration has increased during the Obama administration. Pew Research estimated that there are 3.3 million Muslims living in the US today and 5.7 million Jews. However due to massive immigration (10% of all legal immigrants were Muslims from 2010-2015) and more children, Islam has become the fastest growing religion in the US. By 2040 it will be the second biggest religion after Christians, surpassing Jews. (12)

A report derived from information from the 9/11 Commission and the Center for Immigration Studies reveals that, out of 94 foreign-born terrorists operating inside the United States, 59 of them committed immigration fraud before or during terrorist activity. The sharpest increases from the

Muslim world are from volatile countries such as Iraq, Iran, Bangladesh, and Pakistan. Additionally, there are serious concerns about the number of student visas that are granted to young males from these countries. (13)

According to data compiled by the Brookings Institute, Saudi Arabian nationals – who accounted for 15 of the 19 hijackers on 9/11 – were granted more student visas between 2008 and 2012 than all but three other countries. Indeed, Arabic is the fastest growing language on U.S. college campuses and among the immigrant population in general. In his book *Slavery, Terrorism, and Islam*, Peter Hammond wrote a detailed analysis on the proportion of Muslims to the overall population and increased violence and adherence to Sharia law. Unfortunately with the increased immigration of more radical Islamic people more and more girls will be forced to wear the hijab at American schools as a daily reminder of women rights suppression in Islam and so called "honor killings" and female genital mutilation will become more common in the US, the worst form of cruelty against women. Fortunately some brave women like Hirsi Ali are fighting against that. (14)

Social Media Wars

More and more Americans get their news from sources such as Facebook and Google. The Pew Research Center published a study on May 26, 2016, that surveyed 4,600 people and their behaviors. Respondents are increasingly using social media platforms such as Facebook, Twitter, Instagram, YouTube, and even Snapchat to get their news. Based on the study "News Use across Social Media Platforms 2016," 62% of Americans now get their news from social media. Facebook has become the number one go-to source for news among social media sites. According to the study, 66% of Facebook's US audience gets its news from the site. It's an interesting and timely stat, considering Facebook's recent trending-topics controversy, where the social network came under fire when former contractors alleged that Facebook was filtering out some right-leaning news sources. Facebook denied the accusations but ultimately changed how it filters trending topics. (15) The latest Twitter tracking shows the below followership:

Hillary Clinton:	**8.6 million**
Bill Clinton:	5.9 million
Chelsea Clinton:	1.1 million
Bernie Sanders:	2.4 million
Donald Trump:	**11.5 million**
Ivanka Trump:	2 million (tweets are not political, for women who work)
Donald Trump Jr.:	0.6 million

her staff being so many times bigger than Donald Trump's who just did most of his tweets by himself, he is stronger on social media platforms. Her many layers delay her responses which is a problem on Twitter. His tweets are short, unhinged and widely requoted. Hillary Clinton ran into her first fight and lost very publicly when she tweeted "Delete your account" after clinching the Democratic nomination. Trump's response came swift, "How long did it take your staff of 823 people to think that up – and where are your 33,000 e-mails that you deleted?"

THIRD-PARTY ALTERNATIVES

For a long time, there has been speculation about a third-party candidate. First it was Michael Bloomberg, who was entertaining the idea of an independent run but pulled back after surveys showed that he would mainly hurt Hillary Clinton's chances if he were to run. After the Trump nomination became clearer, some Republicans from the #NeverTrump movement were reportedly organizing around a third party and talking to potential candidates, such as Mark Cuban. Now it has become clear that there will be no such effort despite between 30% and 40% of voters saying they would like to have a choice other than Clinton or Donald Trump.

In 2012 the Libertarian Party had the highest vote in its history, at over 1.2 million, under candidate Gary Johnson, the former governor of New Mexico. This year he is running again and stands at 11% in the polls, only marginally short of the 15% needed to qualify for the presidential debates. Johnson believes if he's in the debates, the ticket could collect electoral votes in states such as New Mexico, Utah, Wyoming, or Alaska. His poll numbers seem to be stable; if they hold, he would far exceed third-party candidates such as Ralph Nader (3% in 2000) but still lag behind Ross Perot (19% in 1992). The Libertarian Party would pull away votes from both parties, especially as both major parties are so fragmented this year. (16)

CLINTON'S STRATEGY

Hillary Rodham Clinton has choreographed every statement, every public move and even her family life on becoming the first "Madame President". She wants to be in the history books and has made sure that nothing is left to chance. She has accrued more than 900 staff, political consultants and can count on the majority of media outlets to back her up.

Contrary to her husband, however, she is not a natural campaigner; she pre-selects her interview partners carefully and is a much more scripted candidate.

HER STRENGTHS

*   She has the best campaign machine (funding, consultants, direct marketing, and digital campaign expertise with experts from Silicon Valley)
*   She has political experience; there's no topic she wouldn't understand.
*   Most of the media is on her side and most of the celebrities
*   She has detailed policy proposals; her plans were years in the making and are well laid out.

- Democrats have a national election advantage; 242 of 270 electorates are almost secure.
- She wins on the commander-in-chief question by ten points over Trump.
- She has much deeper pockets than Donald Trump, FEC filings from July 21 show that she has raised $386 million so far vs. Trump's $94 million. She has currently $86 million left, Donald Trump only $23 million.
- Any Democratic Party candidate would now be preferred by the public over Republicans (a change from fall 2015); the Republican Party had a net negative favorability rating of –24% on May 28. (17)
- Obama's approval rating is at 51%, the highest yet in his second term. (18)

Her Weaknesses

- She is a less intuitive politician (self-admittedly) and has a disadvantage in speeches and campaigning.
- She has little or nothing to show in terms of achievements for her years in government.
- Her personality is more that of a staffer than a Type A.
- She insulates herself in a "bubble" and is not open to outside advice, according to many of her biographers and former team members.
- She has integrity issues (Ranging from Whitewater, putting lobbyists on important committees, using BleachBit software to destroy any trace of her emails while bing in the State Department, "Pay for Play" with foreign governments: 50% of all meetings she could decide to take were with Clinton Foundation donors while being Secretary of State)
- She has authenticity issues, using pre-negotiated questions with reporters, and holding no press conferences in 2016 so far to evade press questions.

- There are questions of her judgment (Iraq War, Benghazi, e-mail affair, Clinton Foundation ties with State department).
- Democratic National Committee data leaks exposing confidential emails. Top four democratic national committee people already resigned and more likely to come.
- Demonstrators at Trump rallies (Many of them are violent and throwing stones at police offers while waving Mexican flags and burning American flags. The more coverage they get the more Independents will be inclined to vote for Trump.)

WHAT SHE NEEDS TO WIN

- Unite the party and give Sanders fans (especially young ones) a reason to join her cause
- Solve / steer away from her scandals (since Aug. 25, she launched heavy advertising and speeches calling Trump a racist and "White Supremacist" to keep her minority support and distract from her scandals)
- Keep together the Obama coalition and excite them to guarantee high turnout
    - High support among women
    - Hispanics and African Americans (currently she has 77% of those voters in polls, Trump only 15%)
    - Union support and working-class whites
    - Young people
- Come across more authentic and warm to improve high disapproval numbers
- Show the benefit of another Obama term and why it would help Americans in their lives
- Show her convictions in a more passionate, connecting, and authentic way

* Ensure other fringe parties (Green, Libertarian) don't pull more voters from her than Trump

Donald Trump has started the same marketing approach on her that he successfully applied to his Republican competitors. He has given her a nickname ("Crooked Hillary"), which he repeats as much as he can to achieve muscle memory with the American electorate. This targets exactly the key Clinton demographic and should emphasize her integrity, trust, and likeability issues.

It is true that Trump has a problem among the female electorate, but Clinton has a far greater problem among men.

Her Lines of Attack

* Look at his past statements on women and Hispanics.
* He is too thin skinned ("A man you can bait with a tweet should not be trusted with nuclear weapons")
* He is unfit to be president and would be dangerous, unpredictable, reckless, and irresponsible in foreign policy and as a commander-in-chief.
    * Comments about banning Muslim immigration from certain countries
    * Wants to dismantle NATO
    * Encourages nuclear armament of more states (Japan, South Korea)
    * Endangers relations with Mexico and China
    * Supports Putin and his coziness with Putin raises national security issues
* He does not care about real working-class Americans but only about himself and making money even when the majority of Americans are losing.
* He wants to hide something as he is not releasing his tax returns; either he is not the success story he claims to be, or he has not paid

enough taxes (every US presidential candidate since Gerald Ford in 1976 has released them).

* He is divisive and drives Americans further apart.
* He is supported by the NRA and he is not against banning assault rifles used in many mass shootings

HER STRATEGY

Clinton is trying to "freeze Donald Trump in place" for Trump's extreme statements made in the primaries, where he had to win over only a small segment of the population holding more extreme views. This way, she can try to prevent him from repositioning in a more centrist way ahead of November. She will continue to characterize him as dangerously unqualified, which she will try to show also in the upcoming debates.

Based on her own high unfavorable poll numbers, she uses her super PAC, Priorities USA, do the dirty work of hitting on his character. They have already started with a big advertising campaign reminding voters of the things he has said about women throughout his life. She is attacking him on his foreign relations statements and policies as well questioning his business record and how "successful" he really was as a businessperson.

She knows that she has to carry only the eighteen states all Democrats won in the last six elections since 1992 plus Florida to win. Any state with a large or growing nonwhite population has become more and more difficult for Republicans to win. And Virginia and North Carolina, long Republican strongholds, have moved closer to Democrats of late.

Her biggest risk is that the Donald Trump phenomenon reaches into some of her key demographics and turns some battleground states red, like Pennsylvania or Michigan on top of Florida and Ohio.

The two most important demographics for her to win by as much as possible are Hispanics and women. To improve her likability, she is planning to lead a positive campaign on her role of uniting Americans and signaling to Americans that she can heal the partisan divisions that have gridlocked Washington.

She is also betting big on grassroots effort and her sophisticated digital-advertising machine. Published reports place her volunteer army at upward of ten thousand, and she is said to employ a squadron of paid consultants four times that maintained by Donald Trump. She spent $5 million on technology and data mining, built upon the pioneering digital apparatus of the Obama campaigns, which is allowing her to microtarget swing voters down to their purchasing, reading, and media-consumption habits. Trump is clearly behind in terms of campaign staff of only about a hundred people and a skeletal infrastructure with no sizable communications team, digital operation, or research division. He needs to step up his ground game for sure in the battleground states.

Clinton has not held any press conferences so far this year; part of her scripted and controlled approach. The *LA Times* reported on May 10 that Correct the Record, is spending a million dollars to challenge social media users tweeting and posting negative things about their candidate. (19)

Different from the super PAC supporting her, Hillary Clinton wants to lead a positive campaign and talk about infrastructure investments, helping women and minorities. She also understands that she needs to improve her standing in Ohio and Pennsylvania among blue collar workers and has done a bus tour there with Tim Kaine and Bill Clinton. About Trump, she says, *"He has no ideas about making America great again. He seems to be particularly focused on making himself appear great. We will have to get below the hype. We have to find what the reality is and see if he actually has the level of success he claims to have. He should release his tax returns."* (20)

Clinton spent three times more money in the primaries than Trump. In total she spent $182 million in her primary campaign to beat Bernie Sanders, Trump only $57 million in total to beat sixteen competitors. (21)

She keeps repeating that Trump is not qualified to be president, quoting his temperament and the reactions around the world to his statements, and emphasizing that the president needs a steady hand and make measured and well-informed statements and decisions.

Clinton is clearly going against the core of Trump's brand promise. She has tried to raise doubts about his success as a businessman and whether he really cares about America and the American people or just about him and making money.

Negative Campaigning

Democrat strategists have closely followed the Republican primaries and have seen that despite the #NeverTrump movement throwing everything against him, it has not worked. They started attacking his core premise of being a successful businessman and caring about working-class Americans. US general elections have unfortunately come down to super PACs, organizations founded solely to bundle lobbyists' money and then launch attack ads against issues and candidates they don't like. Those super PACs do nothing else but test TV ads (mainly attack ads) with consumer groups and see what is most effective, meaning most damaging to someone's reputation. They can do this because the Supreme Court gave them basically free rein in terms of collecting money from unions and corporations and using it in US elections in addition to campaign money. It is no wonder that the public has a more negative view of its elected leaders when those organizations exist only to spend huge sums of money to discredit the other side.

Bush was unpopular in 2004 and couldn't risk muddying himself any more. Clinton is now in even less favor with the American public: She has the second-lowest favorability ratings of any presidential nominee in the history of polling second only to Donald Trump. She needs to steer clear of the mudslinger. Her well-funded Super PAC however will be relentless in attacking Donald Trump in the battleground states of Ohio, Virginia, Florida, Pennsylvania, Michigan and North Carolina. The first wave showed Trump swearing, promising to defund Planned Parenthood, assessing a woman's "fat ass," and so on. Super PACs with patriotic names are a convenient tool to discredit an opponent without generating any blowback for the candidate. It is the same Super PAC that successfully portrayed Mitt Romney as a heartless corporate titan in 2012. They launched a $70 million advertising blitz in August in battleground states such as Florida and Ohio.

The main donors are Saim Haban, James Simons and George Soros. They are attacking Donald Trump on temperament, character, and his "selfish legacy of enriching himself at the expense of others." There's evidence that some of the messages against Trump in the Republican primaries did sink in with independent voters. One features Trump University students begging viewers not to trust Trump were effective with independents. Trump will have to fend off those attacks that are targeted this time at voters who are already skeptical of him. (22)

For his part, Trump will do his best to tie Clinton to any advertising paid for by outside groups. Earlier in the week, he tweeted: "Amazing that Crooked Hillary can do a hit ad on me concerning women when her husband was the worst abuser of woman [*sic*] in U.S. political history." He has criticized her for not being more vocal against the mistreatment of women in many Islamic countries and accepting money from governments that mistreat women for the Clinton Foundation. (23)

As Democrats attempt to negatively define Trump in the minds of voters, they may struggle to concretely sum up the supposed dangers of a Trump presidency, especially given how hard the candidate has been to pin down. Trump has defied conservative orthodoxy, and he continually seems to redefine his own positions. That will make it harder to come up with a comprehensive argument against him. Also, given the intense loathing on display for establishment politicians of all stripes this electoral season, voters may reject the argument that Trump isn't presidential. Sure, he's not a typical politician, but that's precisely why his supporters love him. (24)

The Women's Vote

At no time in US presidential history has gender politics played such an important role as in the Trump-Clinton fight. The first reason is that Trump emphasizes and symbolizes masculine values, and the second reason is that for the first time in US presidential history, a woman has been nominated for president.

> During his speech at the NRA convention on May 20, 2016, Donald Trump was explicit about the voters he's reaching out to: "I will say, my poll numbers with men are through the roof, but I like women more than men. Come on, women. Let's go. Come on." (25)
>
> He has every reason to fight for the women's vote. Women have voted predominantly Democratic in all presidential elections since 1992. Only in 1992 (Bill Clinton's first term) and in 2008 (Obama's first term) the winners had a majority among both sexes. 2016 polls suggest that the gender gap could be bigger this year than in any election since 1952. (26)

Hillary Clinton has one big advantage over Donald Trump. She has many popular surrogates to choose from that can campaign with and for her and appeal to different demographics: Barack Obama, Michelle Obama, Elizabeth Warren and Joe Biden can and will all campaign for her intensively this fall.

Bill Clinton's Role in Clinton's Election Campaign

Bill Clinton is a great asset in every Democrat's campaign except Hillary's. He is still seen as very popular with all Americans, but in this election season, that might not help his wife. It will be interesting to see what role he will play as the general election fight heats up. So far the presumptive "first spouse"—or "first dude," as some claim—has been called Invisi-Bill, working diligently in the background to organize funding and support for his wife. His sometimes-angry statements in Hillary's 2008 primary election campaign against Barack Obama have hurt her more than helped her.

Although Donald Trump has attacked Bill Clinton directly in campaign ads over his infidelity and mistreatment of women in the past, Bill kept quiet and did not comment on this. It would be a gift for Trump if Bill were to attack him and therefore sideline Hillary in the conversation and by doing so indirectly convey the message that she is not the real leader running for president. Such a parallel path could easily sidetrack her campaign or weaken her stance as being able to "stand her ground" herself against a perceived bully like Trump. Last time he intervened, Trump called him out as an example of a sexist that was using his position in the White House, which immediately shut down any further discussion.

Elizabeth Warren's Role in the Campaign
It seems that Hillary Clinton asked Elizabeth Warren in mid-May to start attacking Donald Trump on her behalf, while Clinton was busy defeating Bernie Sanders. Warren launched wave after wave of insults at Trump via Twitter. She continues to act as a Clinton surrogate.

Obama's Role in the General Election
His approval rating has reached over 50%, a new high in his second term. He is still battling with Republicans to get a fair hearing for his Supreme Court justice pick and might seem to many as a better choice than Trump or Clinton, based on their high disapproval numbers. Compared to Hillary Clinton, he is seen as much more authentic and trustworthy. Obama's high rating includes support from a majority of independents and women as well as 82% of Sanders voters. It means that he'll be a powerful surrogate for Clinton in the fall election. (27)

Obama will play an uncommonly active role for a sitting president in Clinton's reelection campaign. The mutual dislike between Trump and

Obama is mutual and very personal. So far Obama is the biggest beneficiary of the fierce primary election and upcoming general election battle. The more Clinton and Trump fight and attack each other, the better Obama looks to voters. His popularity has gone up as he looks even more presidential now and can play the role of wise, older statesman in contrast to the two unpopular presidential candidates fighting it out.

However, his whole agenda and the progress he made in his eight years in office are at stake here, so he has a strong and personal interest to prevent a Trump presidency. From his behavior, it is clear that he is worried about Clinton's performance so far and is eager to help as much as he can. The Clinton campaign will employ more and more fear tactics over time, warning the country not to take a risk and using those scare tactics especially with women and minority audiences. Barack Obama and Michelle Obama will both join Clinton's effort, and they will be very motivated to engage, especially with minority communities.

TRUMP'S STRATEGY
Donald Trump's poll numbers came out strong after the conventions and he is even ahead in some key swing states.

HIS STRENGTHS

- He has an authentic persona (style of campaign, language, no teleprompter or prepared remarks—speaks from the heart).
- He has a "tsunami of support," a real movement, with the highest primary votes ever in Republican history, his supporters are very passionate, 5x more people attending his rallies than Hillary Clinton's on average
- He has strong support among independents and high potential to cross party lines.

* He is seen as the forceful outsider who will be able to overcome the partisan gridlock.
* He has an image as a leader and "fixer", decision maker, tough businessman, and survivor, not pandering to others.
* He has a clear theme with "America First" that focuses on big topics: security (military, terrorism, immigration, crime, foreign policy) and economy (jobs, taxes, infrastructure, education, debt).
* He is seen as tougher in foreign policy in a smart way (similar to Reagan's "Peace through strength" approach).
* He connects intuitively.
* He is fearless.
* He has opened the Republican Party by fully embracing the LGBT community.
* He has the opportunity to improve his high unfavorables by showing his softer side (when he flew to Lousiana to help flood victims) and becoming more presidential.

His Weaknesses

* Many Americans believe he has impulse control issues.
* He made some insensitive statements, reducing his appeal (e.g., his statements on an American judge in his Trump University lawsuit being biased based on his Mexican heritage or about the Muslim father speaking at the Democratic convention who had lost his son who was in the US military).
* He comes across as narcissist and self-righteous.
* The Republican Party is not fully united behind him.
* He has much less money for the fall campaign, many Republican donors like the Koch brothers are staying on the sidelines this time.

Here's an interesting example on Trump's resilience against vicious attacks, by Joe Concha:

On May 15, a breathless front page New York Times piece alleging the then-entertainer/real estate mogul's lewd behavior toward women at his beauty pageants goes viral last weekend. Same deal: Wall-to-wall coverage and analysis on cable news and the Sunday talk shows. Said piece is co-written by the ambiguous Michael Barbaro, who owns the mentality of a snarky 23-year-old blogger on Twitter but really, really wants you take him seriously when it comes to his official (and completely misleading) job of political reporter objectively covering the Trump campaign for the New York Times...a leading newspaper that hasn't endorsed a GOP presidential candidate since 1956.

The story appears to be damaging at first. Trump already has enough problems with female voters, right? But then the piece is exposed for what it is (as a partisan hit piece) after Trump's ex-girlfriend featured in the story condemns the report. And guess what happens? His poll numbers drift upward.

The takeaway is this:

1) American voters don't care what someone in the private sector did in their personal lives decades ago.
2) The American media is so loathed right now, so mistrusted, so discredited, they react one of two ways:
   * Shrug with apathy...
   * Or see right through what the media they hold in contempt is attempting to not-so-subtly accomplish: Destroy a candidate by digging up old stuff that either doesn't hold up like the pageant story or is brushed off/chuckled at as Donald Trump simply being Donald Trump.

To Donald Trump's credit, he has mastered what is arguably Hillary Clinton's most notable strengths: Playing the victim and calling out conspiracies designed to destroy him. Hillary points the finger at Republicans for dirty tricks; Trump points the finger at the media... which to many Republicans are seen as extensions of the Democratic Party anyway. And for the latter, time after time, it works. (28)

What He Needs to Win

* Behave in a more presidential manner
* Show his softer and more caring side, showing inclusiveness and empathy
* Has to show that he has grown as a candidate, be able to take the higher road and no longer resort back to the divisive rhetoric
* Let Clinton continue to self-destruct on her big corruption scandal (destroyed emails she should have handed over, "Pay for Play" with foreign leaders between the State Department and the Clinton Foundation)
* Build out more details in his program, especially on economic plans, foreign policy
* Already present names of experts and respected business leaders he would nominate for jobs in his administration
* Improve campaign infrastructure
* Reach out to women, Hispanics, African Americans, young people (which he started with impressive speeches since Aug. 15)
* Show how business acumen and principles can vastly improve our government (ideas, talent)

His Lines of Attack

Donald Trump's attacks go against both, Hillary Clinton and the current Obama administration. His main attack line is that he is the voice of Americans that get no voice, being the parents of children killed by illegal immigrants or of workers that have been sold out as lobbies have bought politicians to support unfavorable trade agreements. He points to Hillary Clinton selling favors to other governments and business leaders to get rich vs. taking care of Americans and their security as Secretary of State.

- Trump portrays Clinton as a typical crooked, dishonest career politician who is all talk, no action
- She has sold out to the big business lobbyists and they own her
- Corruption is at its peak when a Secretary of State can store her emails illegally at a private server, delete 33,000 emails using BleachBit software, putting the US national security at risk, lie about it and still does not face any consequences
- Americans are less safe at home due to the failed policies of this administration
  - More and increasingly deadly ISIS inspired attacks on American soil
  - Execution-style shootings of police officers across the US due to deepened division along racial lines
  - Spiking homicide and shootings in many cities like Chicago, Baltimore or Washington DC
  - Hillary Clinton wants to increase Syrian refugees to the US by 550%
  - She supports sanctuary cities despite many murders committed by illegal immigrants in the US and thousands criminal illegal immigrants ordered deported roaming free in the US

- The World has become less stable due to Hillary's tenure as Secretary of State and the Obama administration. Trump compares Libya, Egypt, Iraq, Syria and Iran before Hillary Clinton became Secretary of State vs. the current state
  - The situation in the Middle East worst ever despite trillions of dollars spent and thousands of American lives sacrificed
  - No success nor strategy against ISIS after two years of bombing campaign
  - The failed response to the attack on the embassy in Benghazi
  - Refugee waves causing unrest in Europe
  - An Iran deal that makes Iran rich by lifting the embargo without much in return
  - NATO is not focused enough on combatting terrorism and members don't pay their fair share
- Economic growth is sluggish, the "real" unemployment rate is high (especially among young African Americans), household incomes are declining and the national debt has doubled since Obama took office
  - Unfavorable trade agreements by Bill Clinton (NAFTA) and Obama (plans to approve TTIP) result in the loss of many well-paying manufacturing jobs
  - China and Mexico are not playing by the same rules when it comes to international trade but will not be held accountable (i.e. currency manipulation)
  - Excessive federal regulation
  - Hillary Clinton wants to raise taxes
  - Infrastructure across the country is in a bad shape
  - She wants to limit the production of American energy that would create jobs and make America energy independent
  - She is protecting teacher unions vs. helping students
  - Obamacare has increased costs and reduced choice for many (more and more insures bail out of it, most recently Aetna)
  - TSA is not working

He will also pivot off the Clinton Foundation and its rumored use to channel money from foreign businesses and leaders to benefit the Clintons. His speech on the Clinton scandals on June 22, 2016:

"The Clintons have made the politics of personal enrichment into an art form of itself. Hundreds of millions of dollars were channeled via the Clinton Foundation for selling favors to foreign governments and businesses. All that was being done while using a private server to hide from the public while endangering the security of our country. And now a corrupt system is protecting her, basically she used the state department as a private hedge fund. Foreign governments had more influence on our government than Americans based on those money flows." (29)

Hillary Clinton's E-mail Affair

This is about Clinton using a private e-mail account and private server instead of her official government account for her correspondence as secretary of state. This was done contrary to what was recommended, and it made her (and therefore America's foreign policy) correspondence vulnerable to hackers, especially from Russia and China. Supposedly a Romanian hacker hacked her e-mails and supposedly also Russian hackers have cracked her account. Although she was not indicted by the FBI her conduct was described by the FBI director Comrey as "extremely careless". Her behavior and judgement makes people question whether she went to those great lengths to hide anything. The State Department's inspector general issued a report end of May that found Hillary Clinton broke government rules with her personal e-mail use. Donald Trump will certainly use the affair to show Clinton's bad judgment, as this could have or has endangered American interests abroad and put our diplomats and other personnel at risk. He will show that her behavior violated State Department rules and endangered cybersecurity, and he will talk about a double standard as other people have had to face tough legal consequences for much less. Independents and Democrats have asked why such a seasoned public servant exercised such bad judgment. Based on some analysis, the reason could be that she walled herself off from alternative points of view.

Peter Beinart wrote a great article on that on May 27, 2016 in "The Atlantic", "In the journalistic reconstructions of Clinton's decision, two things become clear. First, State Department security experts strongly opposed it. Soon after Clinton became secretary of state, they expressed that distress in a February 2009 meeting with chief of staff Cheryl Mills, a longtime Clinton loyalist. In a March memo to Clinton herself, assistant secretary for diplomatic security Eric Boswell wrote, "I cannot stress too strongly…that any unclassified Blackberry is highly vulnerable." The second thing that becomes clear is that these security experts ran into a brick wall of longtime Clinton aides whose priority was not security but rather her desire for privacy and convenience. "From the earliest days," writes O'Harrow Jr., "Clinton aides and senior officials focused intently on accommodating the secretary's desire to use her private e-mail account" and in so doing "neglected repeated warnings about the security of the BlackBerry." In August 2011, when the State Department's executive secretary Stephen Mull broached the idea of replacing Clinton's personal BlackBerry with a department-issued one, Clinton's deputy chief of staff and close personal aide, Huma Abedin, replied that the "state blackberry…doesn't make a whole lot of sense." To longtime Hillary Clinton observers, all this sounds distressingly familiar. In the literature about Clinton's career, the insularity of her staff is a recurring theme. In his biography, *A Woman in Charge*, Carl Bernstein quotes Mark Fabiani, a lawyer in the Clinton White House, as observing that "the kind of people that were around her were yes people. She had never surrounded herself with people who could stand up to her, who were of a different mind." (30)

The latest reports from the State Department and FBI show that there could be more bad news coming for Clinton that Trump can leverage:

- Report she did not use a secure line for her phone calls
- A supposed debate in the Kremlin whether they should release the twenty thousand e-mails they got by hacking a nonsecure server (31)
- Wikileaks plans to release something big in October damaging Hillary Clinton
- More proofpoints showing close ties between State Department and Clinton Foundation and "friends" of the foundation getting 50% of Hillary Clinton meetings she could decide on
- Her using BleachBit to destroy email records

Was Security Compromised?

It's clear that attempts were made to hack the server. In January 2011, a nongovernment adviser providing technical support for Clinton's e-mail system notified her deputy chief of staff, Huma Abedin, that he'd shut down the server because he believed "someone was trying to hack us," according to the report. Later that day, the adviser updated Abedin with the news that "we were attacked again so I shut [the server] down for a few min." The next day, according to the report, Abedin sent out a notice that staffers shouldn't e-mail Clinton "anything sensitive." Four months later, according to the State Department's inspector general's report, two top staffers discussed—via e-mail, it turns out—concerns voiced by Clinton herself that someone might be "hacking into her e-mail." A

Romanian man known as Guccifer pleaded guilty in federal court to identity theft and unauthorized access to protected computers. It was Guccifer's hacking that revealed that Clinton used a private e-mail address in the first place. (32)

THE RESULT OF THE FBI INVESTIGATION

FBI director Comrey concluded his investigation by confirming that Hillary Clinton was "extremely careless with sensitive information". He also confirmed that she did not hand over all emails and that some classified emails were on that private server. However at the same time he said that the FBI would not pursue charges. Just one day before that conclusion AG Lynch had met with Bill Clinton on her plane and was promised a job in an eventual Hillary Clinton administration. It seems like there was a clear double standard applied as many other people had to face charges for similar behavior but with much less critical or sensitive information. It was the first time in US presidential history that a candidate was questioned by the FBI for criminal charges.

Bill and Hillary Clinton's Treatment of Women

When Hillary Clinton accused Donald Trump of sexism and launched TV ads (via the Democratic super PAC) about it, Trump hit back hard in May. First he hit back at rallies and then in interviews and with TV ads as well, that "Bill Clinton was the worst abuser of women in the history of politics. Hillary was the enabler. Some of these women were destroyed, not by him, but by the way that Hillary treated them after everything went down." (33)

In an interview with Trump on Fox News's *Hannity*, Sean Hannity asked Trump, according to a transcript of the show, "For example, I looked at the *New York Times*. Are they going to interview Juanita Broaddrick? Are they going to interview Paula Jones? Are they going to interview Kathleen Willey?"

"In one case, it's about exposure. In another case, it's about groping and fondling and touching against a woman's will," Trump replied. "And rape."

"And rape," Hannity repeated.

"And big settlements, massive settlements," Trump added. "And lots of other things. And impeachment for lying."

"Smearing," Hannity said.

Trump then mentioned Bill Clinton being disbarred for five years in Arkansas. "You know, he lost his law license, OK? He couldn't practice law. And you don't read about this on Bill Clinton," he said. (34)

Of the three women Hannity mentioned, Jones accused Bill Clinton of exposing himself to her at a Little Rock, Arkansas, hotel in 1991, while Willey has accused Bill of groping her in 1993. Broaddrick, alleged in 1999 that Bill sexually assaulted and raped her in 1978. In 1999, Bill's lawyer, David Kendall, called Broaddrick's allegations "absolutely false." Broaddrick, speaking to *Breitbart News* in an article published May 21, 2016, said the *Times* should devote its energy to investigating claims of sexual assault against Bill. Both Bill and Hillary Clinton have refused to comment on the issue during the campaign. (35)

There is another news story about Bill Clinton that adds to Bill Clinton's issues with women. Flight logs showing the former president taking at least twenty-six trips aboard the "Lolita Express" owned by a convicted sex offender. Flight logs show Bill's presence aboard Jeffrey Epstein's Boeing 727 on many trips between 2001 and 2003 that included extended junkets around the world with Epstein and fellow passengers identified on manifests by their initials or first names, including a woman called "Tatiana." The tricked-out jet earned its Nabokov-inspired nickname because it was reportedly outfitted with a bed where passengers had group sex with young girls. "Bill Clinton...associated with a man like

Jeffrey Epstein, who everyone in New York, certainly within his inner circles, knew was a pedophile," said Conchita Sarnoff, of the Washington, DC, based nonprofit Alliance to Rescue Victims of Trafficking and author of a book on the Epstein case called *TrafficKing*. (36)

Clinton Foundation Issues

The documentary *Clinton Cash* was released at the end of July in the US but was first shown at the Cannes film festival. It reports on the Clinton Foundation while Hillary Clinton was secretary of state and where all the money from foreign leaders and foreign businesses went.

There could have been no better setup for the Clintons to make money and wield political influence than from 2008 until 2012. Hillary Clinton was secretary of state of the most powerful nation on earth while her husband was leading the Clinton Foundation, officially a global charity. Foreign governments and business people could get access to the secretary of state either by making big contributions to the Clinton Foundation or by approaching Hillary Clinton and negotiating politically and showing their gratitude by making pledges to the Clinton Foundation or paying Bill Clinton an exorbitant amount of money for speeches. At the same time the Secretary of State insisted on setting up her own private server against the official policies and recommendations to keep e-mails private and deleted many of them. It is the perfect setup for corruption and the Clintons became very rich between the time Bill Clinton left office in 2001 and now. Best of all, as husband and wife, they can never be forced to testify against each other.

There is the example of UBS, where in March of 2009 Hillary Clinton used her role as secretary of state to intervene on behalf of UBS with the IRS to reduce the number of tax accounts by Americans questioned for tax evasion from 52,000 to only 4,500. After that UBS increased its contribution to the Clinton

Foundation tenfold to $600,000 and paid Bill Clinton $1.5 million for speeches. (37)

Another example is a $29 billion weapons deal that Boeing and other US defense companies had wanted to close with Saudi Arabia for some time. Israel was agitated, and it was known that the Saudi royal family led a highly repressive regime, especially against women's rights and executes the death penalty against gays. In late 2011, one year before Hillary Clinton left the State Department, the deal was recommended in the "national interest" by the secretary of state, with Andrew Shapiro mentioning that the deal seemed "personally important" for Clinton. Curiously enough, the Kingdom of Saudi Arabia had donated $10 million to the Clinton Foundation two years before Clinton became secretary of state, and Boeing contributed $900,000 to the Clinton Foundation. (38)

More issues came up about the Clinton Foundation: The Foundation pays men more than women. Male executives at the Bill, Hillary, and Chelsea Clinton Foundation earn 38% more than women executives, according to a Daily Caller News Foundation review of the foundation's latest IRS tax filings. On average, top male executives at the foundation earn $109,000 more than the top female executives with positions in the C-suite. (39)

His Strategy

Donald Trump keeps the policy part of this election very simple. On his website he offers detailed proposals on only seven issues. These are also the issues he always talks about and that distinguish him most from Hillary Clinton. The choice of topics ensures that he addresses all segments of the electorate and touches on topics that some demographics in the electorate will base their decisions on. Here are the seven topics:

* The border wall and how to pay for it
* Health care reform

* US-China trade reform
* Veterans administration reform
* Tax reform
* Second Amendment rights
* Immigration reform

He needs to find a way to counter the two big questions Hillary Clinton and Barack Obama raise about him. The first one is about his inexperience and he will counter that by questioning her judgement. The key topics to proof her bad judgement will be the e-mail affair, the attack on the consulate in Benghazi and the general situation in the Middle East before she took office vs. now and the Iraq War, which Clinton was in favor of when he was against it. Trump talks not only about the trillions of dollars lost for the United States or the thousands of American soldiers killed but also about the millions of Iraqis that lost their lives as a consequence and how all of that led to the current ISIS problem. The Iraq war will also be used by Trump to counter the second question his pundits raise about him when they question his level of emotional maturity and if he should be trusted with the nuclear codes. He will refer back to the Iraq war to make the case that Clinton is more "trigger happy".

He positions himself as the champion of the people, their voice against a system that is no longer working for many Americans. It is easy for him to connect her with the powerful financial lobbies, elite media and the Middle Eastern governments that have funded the Clinton Foundation so dearly.

His pitch is entirely different from the ones from traditional political candidates. Since Reagan the US has not had a candidate that wanted so much change in domestic and foreign affairs. Donald Trump is a real and bold change candidate with many unconventional and new ideas from trade deals, the border wall all the way to foreign policy. He clearly questions the status quo and believes America is tired of politics as usual and wants a real reboot of policies in Washington DC.

The objective of all his statements about Clinton is to draw a clear distinction between a ruthless, crooked career politician that is all talk and a successful, independent, decisive businessman who wants to turn things around.

His goal is to win over Reagan Democrats and some Bernie Sanders fans, and for that he is willing to move even to her left on some topics such as trade deals. It is much easier for Trump to win over some disaffected blue-collar Democrats than for Clinton to win over disenfranchised Republicans. He will run on personality and judgment rather than detailed proposals. He promises to bring in real experts into his administration rather than the traditional career politicians.

He portrays his politics as common sense and himself as a dealmaker and problem solver that will fight for everyday Americans. At the Republican Convention he talked about how his credo will be "I'm with you, the American people" in contrast to Hillary Clinton's credo "I'm with her". His whole campaign is built on strength and success. His family and business serve as a clear illustration of that and his whole campaign was about connecting to the Reagan revolution, from the campaign slogan, "peace through strength" foreign policy all the way to the "silent majority" that he represents and lends his voice to. His favorite words at the Convention were winning, Law and Order, Americanism and "America First".

He is running against some traditional conservative agenda topics, but it did not cost him at the polls at all. He has expressed support for Planned Parenthood, Social Security, Medicare, and progressive income taxes, and he is skeptical of both supply-side economics and free trade.

His pick of Mike Pence as his running mate was a wise choice. The conservative governor combines a humble personality with political experience at the state and national level. Indiana is a successful state economically that has balanced its budget and Mike Pence unites the Party and will convince many conservative voters that were still at the sidelines.

Donald Trump has already included some ideas from the No Labels agenda into his program. No Labels is a bipartisan group lead by Jon Huntsman and Joe Lieberman that has developed policy proposals that have the support of a majority of voters. Below three examples of such proposals:

* Energy independence
* Border security
* Term limits for members of Congress

How He Can Get Sanders Voters

Donald Trump has realized that Bernie Sanders voters' anger is coming out of the same place as that of many of his voters'. He believes that with his message of going against the political establishment, Wall Street, and unfavorable trade deals and of taxing the rich more, he can lure some of them over to his side once Sanders is forced to give up. This is especially true as they feel betrayed by a Democratic primary system that is by nature less democratic than the Republican one and assigns a significant amount of establishment voters to a candidate of their liking even before the primaries, making it very hard for anybody but establishment favorites to win. In addition the leaked DNC emails have shown a preference by party officials for Hillary Clinton. Trump is already going after Sanders supporters, mentioning them in nearly every speech. He is using Bernie Sanders language when he points to Hedge Funds bankrolling her fall election campaign, how Hillary Clinton used a rigged political system for her enrichment and how she used her office like a "hedge fund". Trump and Sanders have many positions in common like a shared commitment for protecting workers and against new wars and on their zeal for an alternative to the establishment. In terms of demographics, there are also some similarities. Sanders won the same share of white Democrats as Clinton; it was the African American and Latino vote that gave Clinton the edge in the primaries. In addition

Sanders won big with independents, which is also where Trump fetched many more voters from. The big question in November will be how many Bernie Sanders voters will go for Hillary Clinton, how many for Trump and how many will stay home.

> Tierney McAfee writes in People magazine on May 23, 2016 about Trump's chances to get Bernie Sanders voters, "As one respondent, a thirty-four-year-old male IT technician, put it, "Bernie and Trump agree a lot on healthcare, Iraq war, campaign finance and trade. I really want to move on to something new, new ideas from outside the box. Maybe Donald Trump can provide that." Another male Sanders supporter explained, "Trump is an obnoxious vulgar blowhard who says foolish things. However, unlike Clinton—but like Sanders—at least he is an outsider who understands that the government and the economy are broken." A fifty-five-year-old female respondent who described herself as a homemaker added, "Both Trump and Sanders are non-establishment candidates who are not bought by the special interests that have control over policy and legislation because of their 'bribes.'" (40)

His Campaign

Kellyanne Conway has replaced Paul Manafort as of August 18 to broaden Trump's reach and focus his message which helped already a lot in the polls. Paul Manafort has replaced the prior campaign manager, Corey Lewandowski on June 20.

How He Can Turn Around the Women's Vote

For Donald Trump to win, he has to turn around the women's vote. He needs to better control his own messaging but also employ all the support from prominent women he can get. Anybody who knows him well can report how he has treated women equally and promoted and supported strong female leaders all his life. It is about identifying those opinion leaders and publishing those stories from women working for Trump or with Trump across advertising, PR, and social media. He needs many more like Omarosa Manigault, who has publicly voiced support for Trump. Ivanka Trump is a great example as well, but such praise is much less credible from family members than from strong, independent female leaders in their own right. Ivanka talked about his leadership on pay equality at the Trump Organization during her speech at the Republican convention.

I am sure he will come up with an action plan to promote women in America that will help to increase the support of prominent women for his campaign. Independent Facebook groups are springing up all over the country, but they need the celebrity, substance, and advertising support to accompany and enforce the message in an authentic way. The hiring of Kellyanne Conway as his new campaign manager on August 18 was for sure the right move.

Burying the hatch with Megyn Kelly helped for sure, and she gave him good advice on that topic as well. She said, *"Trump needs to act presidentially and being less of a bully, which women tend to not appreciate, either. He can improve his numbers with women."* (41)

How He Can Turn Around the Hispanic Vote
Donald Trump hired many Hispanics in his company and actually won some Hispanics over with his proposals to curb illegal immigration and to build a border wall. Those Hispanics realized that it would help them if fewer illegal immigrants came in, as they drag salaries down and, in the case of crime, discredit the excellent reputation for Hispanics in the United States as hardworking, respectful, and family-oriented immigrants doing the jobs many American are no longer willing or qualified to do. Many Hispanics in

the border region with Mexico actually support Trump over his border wall policy as they fear or see the spilling-over of crime into their communities.

However, Trump needs to do more than just posing with a burrito bowl on Cinco de Mayo on Twitter, and he knows that. Many Hispanics aspire to the American dream and one day becoming as rich as Trump, and he needs to tell them how his economic plan will create more jobs and opportunities for Hispanics. In addition, Hispanic testimonials, PR, and advertising will go a long way in combination with emerging pro-Trump groups in the Latino communities. Geraldo Rivera could be such a great spokesperson, and he seems to be open to that as he respects Donald Trump.

Hispanics pose a great opportunity for Trump as they are in principle more conservative and aspire to become rich as him, many of them work in the construction and hospitality industries, and they are not yet won over by Hillary Clinton. However, he should never again rant against any public official based on his/her Hispanic heritage (as he did with the Mexican judge like in the Trump University trial). That is purely wrong and shines a bad light on him as holding grudges, being racist, and being a narcissist. He should talk about topics Americans are interested in and not play the victim in a private business trial. He has already started a new Hispanic Leadership team and actively messages to Hispanics about promoting good schools and making communities safe as well as about reducing minority unemployment.

How He Is Winning with African Americans

Trump does better with African Americans relative to other Republican contenders in the past; he could easily get into the double digits of African American votes as the first Republican since Ronald Reagan. African American GOP leaders believe that his tightened immigration policies, law and order approach to inner city crime plus hopefully an economic boom will do more for African Americans than some of the Democratic proposals.

In mid-August Trump started with specific messaging to African Americans, telling them how he will focus to improve schools and lower crime rates and help unemployment in bad inner cities. He told them that Democrats have taken their votes for granted but failed them despite ruling most cities in America for the past decades and he will change that if they give him a chance. As the "Black Lives Matters" movement is very hateful towards police he tells African Americans that good policing actually saves lives. He emphasized that every American has a right for safety and every child deserves opportunities.

However, Barack Obama will surely do everything he can to prevent Trump from making big headway in the African American community this fall. Hillary Clinton started on August 25 to air massive ads and accuses Trump of racism. She has no proof point whatsoever, only shows some hate groups saying that they support him. Donald Trump responded with showing actual video footage of her with Byrd, a Ku Klux Klan leader where she said that he was a mentor for her.

How He Is Turning Around the Young Vote

Both candidates continue to have a hard time convincing young voters to vote for them: Hillary Clinton due to a lack of enthusiasm for her positions and because young people don't find her authentic, Donald Trump because of his paternalistic style and his statements on illegal immigrants.

Many millennial voters seem to favor Trump if they cannot have Bernie Sanders as they despise the "Clinton machine" and worry about jobs once they finish college. They see Clinton as part of the system, part of corporate power and bureaucracy. Among millennials (twenty-one to thirty-five years) she is now ahead by only three points in the poll taken in late May. (42)

Small Businesses

Many small business owners, CEOs, and presidents of companies have come out to sponsor Trump as they are fed up with an increase in regulations under Obama. More minimum wage laws and overtime regulation, as well as environmental laws and a complex tax code, have contributed to their pain, and they claim now that they are fed up with all politicians.

His Family

Donald Trump's family is a great asset for him. His kids are hardworking kids with good manners and without scandals, successful entrepreneurs in their own right. Despite their wealthy upbringing, they do not come across as spoiled, arrogant, or aloof but as smart, empathetic, family people who are well-spoken and wholeheartedly support their father's campaign. His family was on display at the Republican convention and it was easy to see how Americans could fall in love with them. Especially his older children, Ivanka, Eric, Donald, and Tiffany held powerful speeches connecting Trump family and entrepreneurial values with American values.

Melania would be the first non-US-born first lady in the White House since Louisa Adams, who was in the White House between 1825 and 1829. She changed her name from Knavs to Knauss and is the daughter of an Austrian man and a Slovenian woman. She came to New York City only in 1996 and speaks five languages: German, Slovenian, Serbian, Italian, and English. She came here on a visa, over time got a green card, and has since then been naturalized, keeping a dual citizenship in Slovenia and the United States. She is therefore a living example of and fierce advocate for the legal process of immigration.

Donald Trump Jr. is the humanizing voice in his campaign, and he acts as a surrogate on news shows, talking about the campaign and his father. The three older Trump kids are also well respected business people in their own respect.

Many CNN and Fox News specials have already featured Trump's wife and kids and showed an idyllic and supportive family that want their father to bring positive change to America. For many of his voters and for sure for many prospective voters, his family is a welcome indication that he also has a mild side, is empathetic, and is not always the tough, cursing, and hardened salesman. It helps also to calm many concerns about him being too extreme or authoritarian and could also help to differentiate him from the Clintons.

Especially for Hispanics and women, his family will be helpful to convince them to vote for him. Ivanka is well known for being an outspoken mentor for female professionals and for going her own way.

The Role of the Media

As highlighted in the section about his primary campaign, this might be the first presidential election in history in which negative campaigning backfires on those who do it.

While McCain and Romney never really fought back against aggressive left-wing media, Trump's strategy is very different, and he fights back on every accusation as swift and hard as possible. Trump knows how to either use the media or discredits it as being "out to get him," which is made very easy by the many news outlets who publish very obvious hit pieces without enough substance or facts to back them up.

His Victory Map

Based on Dan Balz analysis in the *Washington Post*:

> Since 1992 Democrats have always won the same 18 states plus the District of Columbia which account for 242 electoral votes giving them a more than solid base to reach the needed 270 votes. Donald Trump's only path to victory lies in breaking apart

some of those traditional blue states in the Midwest. States like Michigan, Wisconsin or Pennsylvania voted Republican when Ronald Reagan was president but never since. Along with Ohio, Iowa, and Florida, these heartland states are the most intensely contested battlegrounds in the country in the Trump-Clinton race as they have high concentrations of white voters, including large percentages of older, white working-class voters. Donald Trump is appealing to those voters with his campaign focused on better trade policies to bring back manufacturing jobs as well as tighter immigration policies. Virginia should be solidly in Camp Clinton thanks to the nomination of Tim Kaine as her VP. Donald Trump has started to also campaign in Colorado and Nevada but if he cannot make inroads with Hispanics he might focus only on the battleground states in the Midwest plus Florida. Trump's support among white voters without college degrees could be offset by the prospect of similarly strong support among whites with college degrees for Hillary Clinton. The below map is the targeted map by Donald Trump, and it will deliver a slight majority of 273 electoral votes. It assumes he loses all of the southwestern states, with the exception of Arizona, due to his rhetoric and poor numbers in the Hispanic community but that he will win in Florida, Ohio, and Pennsylvania but lose in Michigan, Virginia, and Wisconsin. (43)

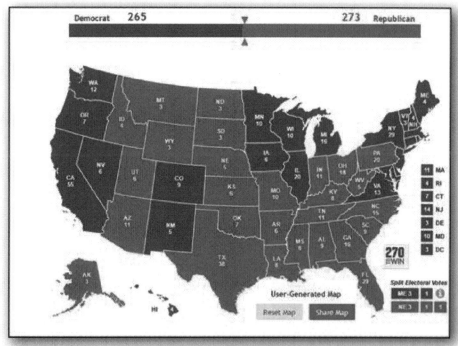

Source: 270towin.com

WHAT THE REPUBLICAN ESTABLISHMENT DOES NOT GET

Many in the Republican Party establishment are still holding back their support for Donald Trump instead of embracing the opportunity with his candidacy. Below is a list of reasons WHY all Republicans should support him.

* This Republican primary was the most successful one in Republican history, if measured by voter turnout, and Donald Trump was the reason. More people turned out for him and more people against him, as nearly 30 million voters casted their ballots this primary season. That's 10 million more than in 2012. Trump won 13.4 million votes, more than any other Republican in a primary in history.

- Trump's inconsistency on ideology should be seen as adaptability and some of his positions are more popular than traditional Republican positions.
- Populism and a positive nationalism could energize, unite, and broaden the party.
- The party can learn from Trump how to modernize its ideology, campaign, and media strategy as well as its outreach to voters.
- Donald Trump is no airhead but a disciplined and successful businessman.
- Only Trump has the means and ruthlessness to fight Hillary Clinton effectively.
- The Trump campaign is a good catalyst to reunite the Tea Party with the party establishment.

Principled conservatives should not try to distance themselves from Donald Trump but learn from Trump how to connect with voters and how to win new. The focus on economic empowerment especially could become a new theme that can convince Reagan Democrats to rejoin the Republican Party. They should learn from Trump how to manage social media and how to come up with commonsense principles when it comes to immigration. Securing the borders and pausing the Syrian refugee program are both commonsense topics. (44)

One thing the Republican establishment seems to miss is that Donald Trump is a calculating businessman who knows what he is doing. Most of what he has said and done was part of his strategy to get a lot of free media, build a loyal and excited base, and force his topics and campaign upon the other primary candidates in the most effective campaign he could wage. Trump drinks no alcohol and works hard as cutting deals is not for the faint of heart and takes a lot of intelligence. Building and successfully maintaining a company like the Trump Organization, with assets around the world and over twenty-two thousand employees, is a major undertaking, and he has managed all that on top of writing books, having a very successful TV show, and building a great family.

Republicans were talking about their need to find a way to expand their shrinking base and appeal more to independents by adapting their ideology, their campaign technology, and their messaging and media use to the new realities to be successful again at the national level. Now somebody has done this job for them, and it's their Republican nominee. Despite any shortcomings many Republicans might find with Donald Trump, they should embrace some of this innovation for their own gain. It's no accident that some of the best innovation comes from new start-ups rather than the existing behemoths, and politics is no different. Trump is a unique chance for the Republican Party to see the future of political campaigning and apply the best of what's working for their future campaigns and connections with the media and a broader public.

Independent of Donald Trump, the Republican Party was already fragmented and has even been split between the establishment and the Tea Party since the 2010 election. If Trump were to win the election, it would confirm a new, winning course, a much bigger and more diverse "tent" for the party. And depending on the results in Congress, it could even lead to the country being in Republican hands from the states to Congress, the presidency, and all the way to the Supreme Court, with the biggest popular mandate for change the country has seen since World War II.

Only Donald Trump is bold enough and ruthless enough to fight gleefully against someone as slick as Hillary Clinton. Kim Strassel from the *Wall Street Journal* commented on that subject:

> That Hillary Clinton has a shot at the White House comes down to one reality: People forget. She is a politician with a lot of baggage. Some wonder how the Clintons despite all of those can still thrive. They've spent decades bulling through their messes, blaming their woes on right-wing plots, and depending on a fickle press and a busy nation to lose interest in their wretchedness. Hillary Clinton once railed that Monica Lewinsky was a "narcissistic loony-tune." It's hard to feel sorry for a woman willing to blame her husband's

dishonor on a 22-year-old intern. The Clintons play hardball but Donald Trump will play smashball; for them, that's new. (45)

Rush Limbaugh makes the case that nationalist populism should be the bigger tent for the Republican Party as it has overtaken traditional conservatism in appeal.

"Nationalism and populism have overtaken conservatism in terms of appeal," Limbaugh said recently. He argues that the formation of the Trump coalition shows conservative ideology is relatively unimportant when it comes to creating conservative voters. "There are a number of Americans who are losers, economic losers, not sad-sack losers. They just lost out in the enterprise of economic globalization that enriches transnational global elites. These Middle Americans see jobs disappearing to Asia and increased competition from unskilled, uneducated, increasing numbers of immigrants, most of them illegal." Such voters, said Limbaugh, are "stuck in the cultural rot brought about by liberalism." However, though they are opposed to the cultural left, they may nonetheless resist the label "conservative" because they do not want cuts to Social Security or Medicare. Trump strongly appeals to such voters with his nationalist trade policy, opposition to illegal immigration, and unwillingness to raise the Social Security retirement age. Trump also has called Medicare "a program that's worked." But Limbaugh also said Republicans have simply failed to respond on what he called the key issue of open borders. (46)

WHO WILL WIN?

In this "election of the century," everything is possible. Most voters are still undecided or flexible, and as both candidates are the most unpopular in US presidential election history, third-party candidates can still have an impact on a tight election. In addition, there are still many topics overshadowing this election that could have a big impact on voter. As always, any big outside event can change the dynamics as well, be it a terrorist attack or a big change in the way the economy is doing.

HILLARY CLINTON WILL WIN IF...

* Donald Trump self-destructs
* Trump antagonizes women again (including female reporters) and Hispanics.
* Trump raises further doubt about his emotional maturity.
* She clearly wins the debates or is seen as equal.
* She manages to stay at least five to ten points ahead of Trump in the commander-in-chief question.
* Trump's tax returns reveal a bombshell, or his record as a successful businessman is seriously damaged.

Most political analysts, media outlets, and prediction markets or models predict a clear Clinton win in November. One of those models is run by Moody's Analytics and predicts a Democrat will win the White House. The reason a Democrat will win isn't about polling or personalities; it's about economics, says Moody's. The economy is the top issue in just about every election. When the economy is doing well, the party currently in office usually wins again. When the economy is tanking, Americans vote for change. So far the US economy is chugging along. Growth (a mere 1.2% GDP growth in Q2, 2016) has slowed but home prices are rising, and gas is cheap. All of this favors Democrats. (47)

Donald Trump Will Win If...

* He can show that he has grown and learned as a candidate, dramatically changing his perception among women as a true and believable advocate for them and the issues they care about.

- He makes inroads with Hispanics, African Americans and millennials by serving as an aspiring model for entrepreneurial empowerment and the American dream.
- Hillary Clinton self-destructs by
  - losing big in the debates
  - deleted emails surfacing that are damaging
  - Bill Clinton making missteps during the campaign or getting publicly linked to the Epstein case
  - Even more proof points for "Pay for Play" between Clinton Foundation and State department. So far it's all indirect via the Clinton foundation and then Bill Clinton being invited to give overcharged speeches (3-4x his regular speaking fee) for the same companies or governments Hillary Clinton has helped or talked to.
- There is another major terrorist attack.
- He can establish another layer of perception with voters by showing his softer side and being more kind, caring, and empathetic. He started that already successfully in mid August by traveling to Louisiana and help flooded areas.
- Emerging third-party candidates steal more of Clinton's votes, and therefore he can win more states.
- He presents a comprehensive program (similar to the 1994 "Contract with America") that Americans approve, or he pledges to take on most of the No Labels policy proposals, including proposals that will help women and Hispanics.

Some voices believe that Donald Trump can and will win. While most Americans trust neither Trump nor Clinton, they give Trump a lot of credit for his authenticity, which does not mean that they like him.

Robert Reich, part of the Bill Clinton administration as secretary of labor and author of many books describes why nobody should underestimate Donald Trump's chances:

A Latina-American from Laredo, Texas tells me she and most of her friends are for Trump because he wants to keep Mexicans out. She thinks too many Mexicans have come here illegally, making it harder for those here legally. A union member from Pittsburgh says he is for Trump because he'll be tough on American companies shipping jobs abroad, tough with the Chinese, tough with Muslims. A small businessman in Cincinnati tells me he's for Trump because "Trump's not a politician. He'll give them hell in Washington." Robert Reich sees Donald Trump as a new kind of politician, which is why political analysts could not have predicted his rise. He calls it the "anti-politician" where it is no longer about right or left and the presidential aspirants moving toward the center once they clinched the nomination. He quotes one Midwesterner, "He may be a jerk, but he's our jerk."

Being seen as a politician might be Hillary Clinton's biggest handicap. Many Americans seem to be skeptical of well-crafted speeches and detailed policy proposals. They prefer authenticity. They want their candidates unscripted and unfiltered. Donald Trump has perfected the art of anti-politics at a time when the public detests politics. (48)

Another voice that predicts a Donald Trump win is Rohit Sharma. He predicts that Donald Trump will win based on below reasons:

* Trend of contrasting personalities: David Axelrod, chief strategist of Obama's 2008 campaign, has a theory that in American politics, incumbent presidents are replaced by incoming presidents who are polar opposites in personality. The careful and aloof George Bush was replaced by the charismatic, connectable Bill Clinton. Then came George W. Bush, who was goofy and a gullible puppet in the hands of his cunning advisers. Then came Obama, an overcautious Bayesian follower and an insular/introverted president who never let others read his mind. Here comes Trump, who is the polar

opposite: he is vocal and loud, and others can read his mind by his words before he even thinks.

* Bold leaders and elevator pitches: Americans love bold leaders who can give great speeches, thump the table, use rhetoric in their engagements, and clearly outline a direct and brute-force path to achieving something. During campaigning, people just want to hear loud and sexy solutions (any solutions).

* Selling to pain: Trump is using a time-tested strategy to market to his early adopters, Americans who feel a loss of pride due to the relegation of United States from the world forum. The pain is a consistent sense of loss of influence and pride, and Trump's "Make America Great Again" slogan effectively sells to the pain of the bruised early adopters. Never underestimate the power early adopters wield over the populace. They start as a minority and can make a concept/idea/person that everyone else was ignoring go viral. (49)

In terms of historical patterns and what they tell us about the result of this election, in theory those would favor Republicans. In seven of the last nine elections, voters have decided to switch the party controlling the White House when a candidate (or his successor) has won two prior elections. Part of the trend could date back to the FDR era, when Presidents Roosevelt and Truman, both Democrats, held office for a combined twenty years. The Twenty-Second Amendment, which limits a president to two terms or ten years in office, came as a direct consequence of that era. (50)

PREDICTION

It is hard to make predictions as the election can swing either way easily. However, despite inherent strong advantages for Hillary Clinton, I believe Donald Trump will win the election.

Donald Trump is riding a real movement that is not losing any steam even more than one year after its start. He has more potential to grow over the next weeks and change perceptions about him. He has the ability to cut across party lines (like Reagan in 1980, Clinton in 1992, and Obama in 2008), personify economic empowerment, bring new approaches in foreign policy, and make proposals how he would make government more effective and entrepreneurial.

Hillary Clinton's "Pay for Play" scheme in the State Department in co-operation with the Clinton Foundation gets more and more unraveled and even Wikileaks has announced more devastating leaks for her in October. Existing leaks have already prompted 4 of the top DNC managers to resign.

While Hillary Clinton has seemingly insurmountable advantages like more campaign funds, popular surrogates (Obama, Biden, Warren) and most of the media support it is exactly those assets in combination that could backfire in an election year where the majority of Americans is fed up with ideology, scripted politicians and a biased media.

He would win the Rust Belt states (Michigan or Pennsylvania) plus Ohio, Florida, and North Carolina based on his focus on the right top-ics like immigration, trade deals and a consistent foreign policy and be-come more presidential.   He would fare better with Hispanics, African Americans, and women than currently expected. They want a stronger, more coherent foreign policy strategy, and the aspirations of working-class Americans (across all races) to fulfill their American dream. In this current atmosphere of anti-politicians, voters will not vote for Hillary Clinton if they have a viable alternative.

The key reason for him winning would be that in the US political landscape in 2016, the left-right political denominations have changed for the middle class everywhere in America, except in Washington, DC. They have been replaced by up and down. Voters now believe that the people above them are getting all the breaks, the people below them are getting all the handouts, but nobody is representing them anymore. Trump has promised to lend his voice to those people.

CHAPTER 3

President Trump

———

THIS IS NOW THE PART of the book where IT has happened. The biggest surprise in US political history has been pulled off. Everyone needs time to digest what just happened and the consequences. History has been made as for the first time ever, someone without any prior political or military experience has been elected to become the forty-fifth president of the United States and leader of the free world.

Half of America is shocked while the other half is celebrating. Wall Street will move sideways or slightly up. Most world leaders will be anxious, and the congratulation messages from world leaders will trickle in to Trump Tower only reluctantly.

This is the part of the book where we leave the analysis (Chapter 1: The Trump Phenomenon Explained) and reporting of current events with some predictions (Chapter 2: Clinton vs. Trump) and enter unchartered territory of speculation. As 2016 has shown so far, the politics of our country have become the most unpredictable ever, and this is even truer if Donald Trump becomes the next US president; anything can be different from what I am writing here. My predictions are based on the latest updates from the campaign trial, the news, and political commentators, on Trump's program, website, books, and speeches, and on commentary of political analysts. In addition I looked at his history of political beliefs, outside policy proposals, the polls in the United States on certain issues, and for which policies he would need the support from Congress on.

As with other topics in this book, I appreciate any feedback and discussion. At the back of the book, in the afterword, you will find information on my website as well as my contact information.

THE TRUMP ADMINISTRATION

Donald Trump has made optimistic pronouncements about making government function more like a business. He would transform the White House into the world's highest-profile improvement club. (1)

Chris Christie is already preparing the transition team; he is an experienced politician who will ensure that a team of experts will be ready to take over government. Most likely a team of five to six hundred people will be recruited to take over the key roles. Donald Trump has already published a list of judges he would nominate for the Supreme Court. Other people on his team would most likely be Newt Gingrich, and for secretary of state, John Bolton could be in play. Ben Carson could become secretary of health and human services. Rudy Giuliani is already leading a committee for Trump to look into immigration issues, so it could well be that he will become America's next secretary of homeland security. Chris Christie and Jeff Sessions could be also members of his administration, and possibly Sarah Palin. There could also be a position for Marco Rubio or John Kasich. Trump would also recruit a record number of business executives for his team, among them could be Carl Icahn, Jack Welch, or Peter Thiel, a big supporter of Trump. Trump will assign a team of business executives to lead trade negotiations on behalf of the United States.

In general the Trump administration would have many more executives from private industry, which, on the positive side, could be refreshing but might also lead to conflicts with existing personnel.

THE FIRST HUNDRED DAYS

Trump's inauguration will be very different from Barack Obama's inauguration. There will be demonstrations, and some members of the so-called political establishment will not be present. Donald Trump will most likely attend only one or two inaugural balls and then immediately start with the work. He is widely expected to show off the new spirit of government in terms of being lean and effective in everything he and the government do.

He will immediately switch into high gear following the inauguration. In the first ten days after his inauguration, he will accomplish these things:

- Send a recommendation for a Supreme Court justice to the Senate
- Ask for confirmation of his cabinet
- Start design work for the wall and bilateral talks with Mexico
- Repeal Obama's executive order on immigration
- Repeal Obama's executive order on more gun background checks
- Start with a symbolic first step to repeal Obamacare
- Tell Pakistan to release Shakil Afridi, the doctor that is in prison there for helping the Americans to find Osama bin Laden
- Start formal and informal conversations about new relationships with Israel, Russia, and Egypt, a key part of those conversations being the alignment on how to defeat ISIS as fast as possible (2)

The open question will be, how fast and how consequent he can be to downshift from hot rhetoric to the serious business of building a presidency based on sound judgment and necessary coalition building.

In those first weeks in office, he will make sure to show how the Trump administration will use American power differently internationally, and he will also prepare to shake up the UN. His team for trade negotiations will also start with new negotiations on trade deals.

Donald Trump will already have transitioned the leadership of the Trump Organization to his three older children, Donald Jr., Eric, and Ivanka.

His agenda for the first hundred days includes these items:

* Start construction on the border wall
* Get his cabinet approved by Congress
* Get confirmation of new Supreme Court justice
* Repeal Obamacare with Congress if both chambers still remain in Republican hands
* Engage Congress in defunding sanctuary cities across the United States, keep deportations of illegal aliens at the same pace as Obama did or slightly higher, and maybe work with Congress on an immigration bill
* Ask for a new screening method to prevent immigrants that believe in Sharia law from entering the US
* Establish a commission to explore how to support reformist voices in Islam and how to spot signs of radicalization earlier of Muslims in the US
* Directly engage in negotiations with companies planning to outsource manufacturing to China or India
* Let his Department Heads provide a list of wasteful spending projects that can be eliminated
* Plan a personal meeting with Putin and Netanyahu

LEADERSHIP STYLE

Many things have been written about Trump's leadership style. Most of those descriptions are, however, either overly boastful or smearing, written by true fans or by hypercritical journalists. Here I am trying to compare some of the positive and negative descriptions and add new dimensions.

POSITIVE VIEW

Edward Luttwak, a famous strategist who consults for leaders and governments around the world on strategy, made a positive prediction about

Trump's leadership as president in an article in the *Wall Street Journal*. He called the fear of a Donald Trump presidency an unjustified phobia that reminded him of the Reagan years. Before Reagan became president, many people feared that as president, he would start a nuclear war and was therefore a threat to human survival. The only war Reagan fought was the invasion of Grenada. He was the president to start peace talks and nuclear disarmament. Edward Luttwak tells Americans that they rather might be up for as good an administrator of the public weal as he was in his presidential campaign—the cheapest by far, and successful too. (3)

Donald Trump's leadership is unquestioned when it comes to entrepreneurship and promoting economic empowerment. He is empathetic, pragmatic, and adaptable. He has the ability to take punches and get off the mat again thanks to fortitude and ingenuity. He is driven and a good team builder. All that is according to someone who has worked with Trump closely now but was against him before, Anthony Scaramucci. (4)

Among the leadership traits that Donald Trump would bring with him to the presidency are impulsivity, bravado, unpredictability, hype, and flexibility. (5)

The journalist Dickerson was asked if Hillary Clinton was being more vindictive or Donald Trump. The question clearly caught Dickerson off guard. "Oooooo. Man, I don't—I don't know. I think Clinton," he said finally. "Trump is very tough on those he does not like, as I know. But he gets over it." (6)

Trump employs a lot of women in high positions in his company; he has an eye for talent and is happy to recruit people who show their abilities by opposing him. Inside his organization they are paid well and enjoy a level of autonomy equal to the pressure he places on them. Success depends, at least in part, upon showing dedication and toughness the boss can respect." (7)

Negative View

The most commonly held negative views about Donald Trump's leadership are about him being not emotionally mature enough and too narcissistic.

Personality-wise he is someone who likes the hunt, the campaigning, the "getting it," so it has to be seen whether he will still be highly motivated about governing versus campaigning for US president.

Trump's exuberance is often so great that someone could imagine a little boy who is desperate for approval and has never been told that bragging is obnoxious. He keeps his magazine covers framed and displayed on a brag wall in his office. (8)

On September 26, 1981, Donald's older brother, Freddy, died of alcoholism at just forty-three years old. It was a formative and defining episode in Donald Trump's life. In Donald's view, "Our family environment, the competitiveness, was a negative for Fred." However, Donald also seemed to blame his brother for letting others take advantage of him. He was, in other words, a sucker. "Freddie just wasn't a killer," said Donald, and he didn't defend himself, which was "a fatal mistake." Fred's death had taught Donald "to keep my guard up, one hundred present." (9)

Trump has a unique talent as a salesman and brags about being able to convince others that he knows as much about a subject as them. Asked how he manages this trick, Trump said, "It's a feeling, an aura that you create." In another bit of reflection, Trump revealed himself to be defended even against self-evaluation. "When you start studying yourself too deeply, you start seeing things that maybe you don't want to see." (10)

IS HE AUTHORITARIAN?
He is a fighter, and people like that about him. The left has called him racist, sexist, xenophobic, and authoritarian. Everybody who knows Donald Trump or who has worked for him says he is not; in fact he really treats everyone the same, and his actions speak louder than his words.

The most important question to clarify is how he would treat that enormous power once he became US president. The United States was built and founded upon strong principles that should prevent from ever falling under authoritarian rule. This question is very important for all Americans and among the harshest arguments against Trump.

Hillary Clinton is telling people that she fears that Trump would act like a dictator once elected, to stoke fears about him being authoritarian. Arguably, he has shown some authoritarian tendencies in his conduct with hecklers and the press, in his answers to Republican debate questions on torture and how he would ensure soldiers would follow his orders when asked to do something immoral. Would he use the means of the administration and executive power to go against his enemies?

In my view, the United States has strong institutions and a clever electorate. Most of all, the system has strong safeguards to limit the president's power as no other democracy in the world has. Not only would Donald Trump not act authoritarian, but also our institutions and his own party would not allow that. The safeguards in place are the following:

* Strong, free, independent press: print, TV, online
* Congress with power to impeach
* Military sworn to defend the Constitution, not the president
* Supreme Court
* His own family
* His own popularity at risk, which would sink with behavior like that
* Election every four years as mandated by the Constitution

HIS EMPATHY

One aspect about Donald Trump that has not yet received any or enough coverage is his employee relations. He has helped so many people throughout his career with advice, money or by providing great opportunities. He employs over 22,000 people at the Trump organization, a business success like no other US president had before. He provided great and equal opportunities for women and minorities. He would for example cut out tragic stories from newspapers and individually contact those people going through losses and help them.

Many friends of Trump and others who know Trump personally told *People* magazine that offstage he is "caring and kind". British journalist and *The Apprentice* alum Piers Morgan said he is "far more thoughtful and measured," in reality. "If you are in Donald's camp and you are good to him, he's unbelievably good," says Piers Morgan. He has made insensitive and sometimes inflammatory statements, but by judging his actions, someone gets a very different picture:

- Omarosa Manigault credits him with financing her idea for a minority version of *The Bachelorette* and letting her take it to an all-black network. "When it comes to diversity," she insists, "he puts his money where his mouth is."
- A Jewish member of Trump's Mar-a-Lago club in South Florida credits him with "really opening Palm Beach to the Jewish population."(11)
- Robin Bernstein says he is truly supportive of women, like the time he realized that the LPGA winner's prize of $215,000 at his Trump International Golf course was far below what a male golf champ would win, so he raised it to $1 million. (11)
- Trump offered Obama adviser David Axelrod his help in 2010 to plug BP's massive deep-sea oil leak in the Gulf of Mexico. Trump followed up, Axelrod recalls, with an offer to build for the White House "a beautiful modular ballroom" to replace "what he called 'these s…ty little tents' the Obamas were using for state dinners on the South Lawn." Even after being snubbed on both offers, Trump donated $100,000 to the Axelrod family's epilepsy-research charity.

* Donald Trump hosts events at Mar-a-Lago for wounded Iraq War veterans. (11)

Trump's first bodyguard/chauffeur, Robert Utsey, recalled him as considerate, generous, and sincere:

When I got married, he came to the wedding and gave us a nice present, which he didn't have to. When my wife was pregnant, my wife chose a doctor who wasn't in the medical plan, but he paid or it, which was about a month's salary. When the baby was born, he bought the car set that we brought her home in. He was a nice guy who was never anything but good to me. He expected loyalty but he was also loyal back. The guy I knew was a good guy. (12)

Golf player Natalie Gulbis says this about Donald Trump in an article on golf.com:

I have found him to be gracious, generous and inspiring. He encouraged me to look at myself as a brand and as a professional golfer with a huge platform to grow the game of golf, regardless of my gender. He offered me a simple idea that changed my life forever. We talked marketing and business. He has a way of cutting through small talk and digging into areas where he can have an impact. When he asked me about my goals—which would become a recurring theme in future conversations—his advice was simple: "Never fear challenging the status quo." Not only does that advice seem to be something he is following with great success in his campaign, but it's also something I've taken with me to the sports marketing world. Donald was adamant that in endorsement deals I should request and fight for equal pay that man were receiving. As you can tell, he has had a tremendous impact on me, both as a female golfer and an entrepreneur. He's helped me think of new ways to grow women's golf, advised me to never accept the first offer, and emphasized time and again that there's room for women's golf in a crowded sports world.

I last saw Donald at the 2015 Women's British Open at Turnberry. He was also interested to hear about Lydia Ko—our top ranked player. "What makes her so good?" he asked. As usual, he wanted to know more about winners. That never-ending desire to learn more about and from the best in any field, that's the Donald Trump I know. (13)

There's no question that Donald Trump also has a much softer and more empathetic side he would also get to show more as US president. "Trump has a much broader array of emotions than people know. The image he has created is so egotistical and not friendly, and he really is the opposite in many ways," said James Dowd as he and Mark Burnett got to know Trump really well thanks to filming *The Apprentice*. Bill Rancic recalled most vividly an encounter he witnessed between Trump and a boy of perhaps ten who had terminal cancer. The boy was a fan of the program *The Apprentice* and wanted to be "fired" by Trump. A charity called the Make-A-Wish Foundation arranged a meeting, and the boy dressed in a suit and tie and rolled a suitcase into the boardroom set of *The Apprentice*. (The show requires that contestants who are dismissed be filmed departing with a wheeled suitcase.) As Rancic tells the story, Trump shook the boy's hand, listened to his request, but couldn't bring himself to utter his signature line "You're fired." Instead he gave the boy a check for several thousand dollars and said, "Go and have the time of your life." The reserved Trump who couldn't fulfill a boy's dream to be fired was nowhere to be seen on edited broadcasts of *The Apprentice*. Instead, viewers who tuned in got a nonstop display of his ego. (14)

Domestic Policy

Democrats and Republicans will have to find a way to work together, no matter how the election in November ends. If they don't, America will fail. For the last decade, America has benefited as global investors poured a lot of money into our currency and companies because the rest of the world looked so bad in terms of investment opportunities. This won't last forever. America's problems—ranging from exploding debt and a crumbling infrastructure to incomprehensible tax and regulatory systems—are deadly serious. Millions of people are still out of work, working part time when they'd rather be full time, taking low-paying jobs for which they are overqualified, or giving up looking for work altogether. At the root of our problems is the refusal of our leaders to seek common ground. Our next president's most important task is to bridge this divide, with a real plan to bring the parties and the nation together.

No Labels, the growing movement of Democrats, Republicans, and independents, has such a plan. On April 21, 2016, it released a book called the Playbook for America's next president, an ambitious blueprint for bipartisan problem solving. No Labels has developed an agenda that represents both good politics and good policy. Through nationwide polling and workshops with policy experts from across the political spectrum, the organization sought to identify America's most pressing challenges and develop policies that make sense, that our country can afford, and that the American people can support. No Labels developed a playbook of sixty concrete ideas designed to progress toward four goals: create twenty-five million new jobs over the next ten years, secure Social Security and Medicare for the next seventy-five years, balance the federal budget by 2030, and make America energy-secure by 2024. The vast majority of ideas garnered between 60% and 80% support in polls.

For example, there's an idea to sunset and reconsider all federal regulations after fifteen years and to create a regulatory roadmap that enables entrepreneurs to view in one place all the federal, state, and local regulations that may affect their businesses. There's a recommended radical simplification of both the corporate and individual tax codes. There's also a suggestion to reimagine the Community Reinvestment Act—which provides incentives for banks to lend to people in low- and moderate-income neighborhoods—to allow more funding to be funneled to start-ups there.

The research has shown that America is not hopelessly divided, as cynics and ideologues might have us believe. In fact, there are many credible ideas that address voters' most significant concerns and appeal to a broad swath of Democrats, Republicans, and independents. No Labels has built a million-plus-member citizen army and empowered a "problem-solver caucus" in Congress that now numbers almost eighty members.

As Washington's dysfunction is directly harming the health, wealth, and well-being of American families, it is time to find new approaches to solve our problems. Here are some examples:

* Retraining the unemployed (mandatory vocational and reemployment training for the long-term jobless)—82% support among American voters in polls
* A regulatory "sunset" (all regulations would expire after fifteen years unless Congress renewed them)—68% support
* More revenue for Social Security (Increase payroll taxes by 1% and raise the maximum taxable income threshold)—63% support
* Infrastructure bank (a new public-private partnership to fund infrastructure projects)—62% support
* Simpler corporate taxes (reduce the corporate rate to 25% and eliminate most deductions and credits)—62% support (15)

TAXES, BUDGET, AND DEBT
Donald Trump's tax plan is similar to Ronald Reagan's as he would slash regulations dramatically, reduce the corporate tax from 35% to 15%,

increase the tax on the richest Americans and invest a lot in US infrastructure and the US military. On the US minimum wage he was first opposed to any increase, and then he said he would leave it to the states but lately indicated that he would not be opposed to an increase. Donald Trump will try to simplify taxes dramatically and that would be a big progress for all Americans and companies doing business here.

* Offer tax relief for the majority of Americans (working poor and middle class)
  * Americans would pay 12%, 25%, or 33% (three instead of the current seven brackets); no more marriage penalty or alternative minimum tax; charitable giving still deductible, but most other deductions to fall, enabling a much simpler tax return
  * No more death tax
* Simplify the tax code
* Discourage corporate inversions (16)

He argues that this tax plan will be paid for by the following:

* Offer a one-time repatriation deal, like a 10% tax rate, on all cash bunkered outside the United States. Currently US corporations have $2.1 trillion stashed overseas to avoid high taxes in the United States. (17)
* Eliminate all loopholes and deductions in the tax code for the rich. This would be an area where his expertise as a billionaire who knows how to save taxes would be helpful rather than having a politician at the helm.
* Reduce and eliminate corporate loopholes. (17)

So far his Trumponomics approach seems to be a much simpler and more growth-driving tax code than exists currently, with low taxes and high infrastructure spending at a time of low interest rates, but the Federal Reserve would have to play its part.

Critics have said that some of his economic positions are still leading to an increase in our national debt. (18)

Others have criticized that there are not enough fresh ideas in his economic plan around innovation and new technologies. A very vocal critic of both candidates has been Marc Cuban, who said, *"It's a problem that all the candidates appear to be technologically illiterate. Using or not using e-mail, being on social media, neither reflects knowledge of technology. The future of this country, our jobs, economy, security, culture, lifestyle and more are intertwined with advanced technology. How can you hope to strategize and create solutions to issues we have without having more than a basic understanding of technology? Wars won't be fought with bombs and bullets alone but also with bytes and advanced technologies."* (19)

IMMIGRATION

Donald Trump is very clear that only a country that has a border is a real country and the most important role for the government is to secure that border. This topic was the first that Trump brought up when announcing his run for president, and it created a very loyal fan base from the beginning and helped him surpass all other candidates at that time. He hit a nerve with many Americans with this topic. Trump is for legal immigration—his wife immigrated legally.

His argumentation for the wall: Only one thousand miles of wall is needed. More than two thousand years ago, the Chinese built a wall of over thirteen thousand miles that could never been breached. Walls work; that's why Obama just put a new wall around the White House to keep intruders out and why the Israelis built a wall at $2 million per mile that helped to stem the inflow of terrorists. In Yuma the wall already works and has greatly reduced the influx of illegal immigrants. In his view, a country either has a law or it doesn't. How can you be punished for parking in the wrong spot in NYC while not being punished for entering a country illegally? He also wants new measure against "anchor babies," as birth tourism, especially from China, is exploding. (20)

Donald Trump has also laid out in detail on his website how he would make Mexico pay for the border wall. He would engage them in negotiations and is ready to limit or regulate the $24 billion that Mexican Americans send to Mexico every year if Mexico does not agree to pay one time $5 to $10 billion to build the wall. Trump writes that the current legislation already covers that in the Patriot Act, section 326, and compelling financial institutions to demand identity documents before opening accounts or conducting financial transactions. He would just need to redefine the applicable financial institutions to include money-transfer companies such as Western Union and redefine "account" to include wire transfers. It would include the provision that no alien may wire money outside the United States unless the alien first provides a document establishing a lawful presence in the United States. Mexico would protest as it receives approximately $24 billion a year in remittances from Mexican nationals working in the United States. The majority of that amount comes from illegal aliens. It serves as de facto welfare for poor families in Mexico. There is no significant social safety net provided by the state in Mexico. Trump would tell Mexico that if the Mexican government contributes the funds needed to pay for the wall, the Trump administration will not promulgate the final rule, and the regulation will not go into effect. (21)

The same would be true for trade tariffs. Mexico needs access to our markets much more than the reverse, so we have all the leverage and will win the negotiation. By definition, if you have a large trade deficit with a nation, it means it is selling far more to you than the reverse—thus it, not you, stands to lose from enforcing trade rules through.

Another point of leverage would be the visa. The United States could threaten to no longer issue visas to hundreds of thousands of Mexicans and to important business people and politicians there. Even a small visa fee or a fee on border-crossing cards could pay for the border wall. The border-crossing card is also one of the greatest sources of illegal immigration into the United States, via overstays. Mexico is also the single largest recipient of US green cards, which confer a path to US citizenship. Increased tariffs could also be imposed on Mexican goods if Mexico does not pay for the wall. So Donald Trump strongly believes that the United States has a lot of leverage over Mexico. (21)

Donald Trump and many independent Republicans have long argued that many politicians want immigration reform that would result in amnesty, cheap labor, and open borders for a long time. The reason they want that is because of their campaign sponsors, which are big companies who would benefit from cheap labor at any level. He argues that real immigration reform needs to put the needs of working people first—not wealthy globe-trotting donors.

He says that illegal immigration puts downward pressure on wages for job seekers, and African Americans have been particularly harmed. He also quotes some of the horrific crimes illegal immigrants have committed in the United States and the increased danger of terrorists crossing over from the south. More and more Afghan and Pakistani nationals are trying to come into the United States over that southern border, some of them with terror ties. Even ISIS has reported seeing the southern border as an opportunity to get terrorists into the United States. (22)

Donald Trump says that nobody should be above the law as America has always been a nation of laws. These items are part of his plans for immigration:

* Triple the number of immigration law enforcement.
* Nationwide e-verify to protect jobs for unemployed Americans.
* Mandatory return of all criminal aliens. Since 2013 the Obama administration has released from its custody seventy-six thousand aliens with criminal convictions. All criminal aliens must be returned to their home countries, a process that can be aided by canceling any visas to foreign countries that will not accept their own

criminals, and making it a separate and additional crime to commit an offense while here illegally.

* Detention—not catch and release. Illegal aliens apprehended crossing the border must be detained until they are sent home.

* Defund sanctuary cities. Cut off federal grants to any city that refuses to cooperate with federal law enforcement.

* Enhanced penalties for overstaying a visa. Millions of people come to the United States on temporary visas but refuse to leave, without consequence. This is a threat to national security. Individuals who refuse to leave at the time their visas expire should be subject to criminal penalties; this will also help give local jurisdictions the power to hold visa overstays until federal authorities arrive. Completion of a visa-tracking system will be necessary as well.

* End birthright citizenship. This remains the biggest magnet for illegal immigration. By a 2:1 margin, voters say it's the wrong policy, including Harry Reid, who said "no sane country" would give automatic citizenship to the children of illegal immigrants.

* Requirement to hire American workers first. Too many visas, such as the H-1B, have no such requirement. In the year 2015, with ninety-two million Americans outside the workforce and incomes collapsing, we need companies to hire from the domestic pool of unemployed. Petitions for workers should be mailed to the unemployment office, not USCIS.

* Immigration moderation. Before any new green cards are issued to foreign workers abroad, there will be a pause where employers will have to hire from the domestic pool of unemployed immigrant and native workers. This will help reverse women's plummeting workplace participation rate, grow wages, and allow record immigration levels to subside to more moderate historical averages.

* Put American workers first. Decades of disastrous trade deals and immigration policies have destroyed our middle class. Today, nearly

40% of black teenagers are unemployed. Nearly 30% of Hispanic teenagers are unemployed. The influx of foreign workers holds down salaries, keeps unemployment high, and makes it difficult for poor and working-class Americans—including immigrants themselves and their children—to earn a middle-class wage. Additionally, we need to stop giving legal immigrant visas to people bent on causing us harm. From the 9/11 hijackers to the Boston bombers and many others, our immigration system is being used to attack us. The president of the Immigration Caseworkers Union declared in a statement on ISIS: "We've become the visa clearinghouse for the world." (22)

HEALTH CARE
Donald Trump wants to repeal the Affordable Care Act. He argues that it has resulted in higher costs, websites that don't work, greater rationing of care, higher premiums, less competition, and fewer choices. On day 1 of his administration, he wants to ask Congress to repeal Obamacare. He wants Congress to come up with alternatives. Here are his guidelines for this:

- Modify existing law so that health insurance companies can compete across state lines.
- Allow individuals to deduct health insurance premiums from taxes.
- Allow individuals to use health savings accounts (HSAs), which should be tax-free and allowed to accumulate, especially good for young people.
- Require price transparency from all health care providers, especially doctors and health care organizations such as clinics and hospitals; individuals should be able to shop to find the best prices for procedures, exams, or any other medical-related procedure.
- Remove barriers to entry into free markets for drug providers that offer safe, reliable, and cheaper products; allow consumers access to imported, safe, and dependable drugs from overseas to bring more options to consumers. (23)

DEALING WITH CONGRESS
Mike Pence as VP who will help to get Trump's agenda through Congress. The Republicans will retain control of the House of Representatives and maybe even of the Senate in the November 2016 election.

He will drive an ambitious agenda and will regularly engage actively in meetings with key Congress leaders and try hard to bridge the partisan divide with a mix of charm, deal making, and using the public and media to draw attention to any roadblocks or important issues legislative leaders need to solve. It will be the totally opposite approach of Obama's approach.

OTHER DOMESTIC POLICY

Education
The biggest changes Donald Trump wants to make here is to bring education policy back to the state and even more local level. His program calls for the end of Common Core as it has proven ineffective: the United States is spending the most of any country on education but ranks only twenty-eighth in the world.

Protecting Second Amendment Rights
The right of the people to keep and bear arms shall not be infringed upon says Trump. Period. Trump wants stricter laws to prosecute violent criminals, especially when it comes to gang-, drug-, or gun-related crimes. He praises a program in Richmond, Virginia, where if a violent felon uses a gun to commit a crime, he/she will be prosecuted in federal court and go to prison for five years—no parole or early release. Murders committed with guns in Richmond decreased by over 60% when Project Exile was in place; 350 armed felons were taken off the street in the first two years of the program alone.

He wants to empower law-abiding gun owners to defend themselves. He sees gun ownership as common sense to defend yourself as police cannot be everywhere all of the time.

His strategy against mass shootings is to fix the broken mental health system. He says that all of the tragic mass murders that occurred in the past several years have something in common: there were red flags that were ignored. Treatment programs must be expanded because most people with mental health problems aren't violent; they just need help. But for those who are violent, a danger to themselves or others, we need to get them off the street before they can terrorize our communities. This is just common sense. On background checks, rather than expand the current system, he wants to ensure that it is better working so that it includes all criminal and mental health records. (24)

At the same time Trump has the ability to negotiate some common sense gun laws with the NRA. Donald Trump is already using his bipartisan appeal to find a solution to ban people on the terrorism watch list from buying guns and will talk to the NRA that supports his candidacy about it. 60% of Republicans and 80% of Democrats would support that move.

FOREIGN POLICY

Foreign policy is one of the key topics where Donald Trump and Hillary Clinton differ a lot. The Trump approach is an "America First" approach, which means the United States should be engaged in those conflicts and regions where its own safety and interest or that of one of its close allies is threatened. His foreign policy will be guided not by partisanship or ideology but purely by American interest and common sense. Trump has a lot of fresh and new ideas, and challenges the status quo and reasons why things have been the same way over the past decade. He will not always talk about what exactly he will do next in going against enemies like ISIS or take options off the table as it reduces the chances of success on the battlefield and increases the chances of the enemy to adapt. He intends to use surprise and unpredictability in foreign relations, therefore helping to improve the US positions in all negotiations with other countries, friendly (how to share the burden of an intervention) or hostile (they will not know what to expect).

It is expected that the world will be polarized by Donald Trump's election as well. There will be three camps.

* Possibly better relationship: Israel, Russia, Eastern Europe, North Korea (Kim Jong-un already praised Trump for being willing to negotiate directly)
* Possibly worse relationship: Iran, Pakistan, Mexico, and China
* Same relationship as now to be expected: Western Europe, South America, Canada, Australia, India

Donald Trump has always had a keen interest in foreign policy. As early as in 1987, he spent more than $90,000 to purchase full-page newspaper advertisements in the *New York Times*, the *Boston Globe*, and the *Washington Post*. The headline of the ad announced, "There's nothing wrong with America's Defense Policy that a little backbone can't cure." In the ad Trump questioned America's defense commitments in Europe and Asia and argued that the United States "should stop paying to defend countries that can afford to defend themselves." He added, "Make Japan, Saudi Arabia and others pay or the protection we extend as allies. Let's help our farmers, our sick, our homeless." He said, "I'm tired of watching the US getting ripped off by other countries." (25)

Donald Trump's strategy is to improve our military and ensure that this power is visible. The United States will be safer when the rest of the world believes we have the power and the will to act if necessary. It's the same approach used by George Washington, who once said, "If you want peace, prepare for war." Ronald Reagan also followed the "Peace through strength" approach. At the beginning of his presidency he built up the American military and talked about the Sovietunion as the evil empire. At the end of his presidency it resulted in a reduction of nuclear stockpile and a warming relationship with the former Cold War enemy on American terms.

Rumsfeld summarized in an interview on June 22, 2016 what the new US president should do differently in foreign policy: *"The US needs to act again like a Superpower again. Obama has created a vacuum in the world so the friends of the US are less certain of US support leaving more opportunities for the enemies of the US to do whatever they want. Putin appears so much powerful because he feels free to do whatever he wants to do."* (26)

Donald Trump appears to some as an isolationist, but the term "America First" means for him something else. What Trump means by it is that America will be number one, which is not the same thing for him as isolationism. He will be less warmongering than Hillary Clinton; however, he was not always clearly against the Iraq War or the US intervention in Libya. Initially he gave statements supporting both endeavors. It seems as if he wants to engage only in those wars America can win. Some describe Trump's foreign policy approach as being in the Jacksonian tradition: "Basically focused on the interests and reputation of the United States. They are skeptical of humanitarian interventions and wars to topple dictators, because those are idealistic quests removed from the interests of everyday Americans. But when American interests are in question, or failing to fight will make America look weak, Jacksonians are more aggressive than anyone...With them it is an instinct rather than an ideology—a culturally shaped set of beliefs and emotions rather than a set of ideas." (27)

Donald Trump recently gave a big foreign policy speech on April 27, 2016:

* The United States needs to get out of the business of nation building.
* NATO allies all have to pay their fair shares and not just rely on the United States, or be left to defend themselves.

- He called to "shake the rust off" America's foreign policy.
- He criticized Obama for not using the term "radical Islam."
- He scolded the Bush and Obama administration for making mistakes in Iraq, Egypt, Syria, and Libya, causing the ISIS rise that led to the migrant crisis destabilizing the Middle East and even Europe.
- He wants the United States to project strength and better understand who our real friends and enemies are.
- Russia and China are not bound to be adversaries. (28)

Expected Trump Policy per Continent or Country

Steve Coll from the *New Yorker* has argued that the costs of our military are relatively low compared to what we get for it compared to so many other expensive government programs. Therefore, he believes that Trump's rhetoric around no longer wanting to spend money for the defense of NATO or South Korea and Japan should be seen as a starting point for negotiations, not a desired end state that could make the world and the United States less stable and peaceful:

> "(…) According to the World Bank, the US spends 3% of its GDP on the military. As an investment in shared prosperity (or, if you prefer, global hegemony), the running cost of military power may be one of history's better bargains… Because the US military is so much larger and more effective than any other, and because militaries are so hierarchical, it is more efficient to defend the core alliances disproportionately, from Washington…The security of the European and East Asia democracies has been vital to American prosperity and stability for seven decades, and it may remain so for seven more. The Middle East is another story as besides Israel, Tunisia, and an increasingly illiberal Turkey, none of our allies there are democracies. Since 1967, US forces have intervened half a dozen times in wars in the region, and it remains deeply violent and unstable." (29)

The Americas

In terms of Mexico, we can already see now that the relationship between the United States and Mexico will be off to a hard start based on the measures planned (including the border wall) to stem the influx of illegal immigrants. Over time this relationship should become a productive and effective one in the interest of both countries. The relationship with Canada should be a good one. As for other countries, there will not be much change. In terms of Cuba, Donald Trump will not be in a rush. He will wait until there is real progress in terms of capitalism, freedom, and human rights before reconnecting Cuba and the United States fully again.

Europe

European leaders will have to warm fast to Donald Trump once elected as they need America more than ever. Western European leaders like Hollande and Merkel will not be as forthcoming at the beginning as they all have a preference for Hillary Clinton. In younger democracies in Eastern Europe, there is a much friendlier vibe for Donald Trump as they wish for an American president that behaves less defensively but more like a real Superpower. Irritations should be over soon, and Trump and European leaders will be able and willing again to tackle the big global problems. Europe would also be very relieved if the sanctions against Russia could be lifted as they are suffering more than the US. In Europe, Angela Merkel would be forced to cooperate with Donald Trump and forget their skirmishes during election season and the new British Prime Minister Theresa May after the Brexit will be more dependent on the US "special relationship" than ever. Angela Merkel did not respond to him calling her refugee policy outright stupid and misguided. It will take some time digesting and hiding their real emotions, but there will be a productive relationship, and relations will not deteriorate the same way they did during the George W. Bush presidency after the Iraq War.

Donald Trump could schedule a visit in Kallstadt, where his grandfather's family is, and Melania could visit her family in Slovenia as part of one European visit.

Middle East

This is still the biggest problem region. Donald Trump will develop a plan here on how to best defeat ISIS fast with ground forces from Saudi Arabia, Egypt, and Turkey or he will help the Kurds take over that territory. An alternative could be a coalition of those countries plus up to 10,000 US troops and even Russian troops. Donald Trump will have a much better relationship with Israel and the Gulf states than Barack Obama had.

The United States will most likely continue to support Egypt financially and economically to stabilize the biggest Arab nation in terms of population and at the most important geographic location strategically. Donald Trump has also said that he will also try to negotiate a peace deal between Israel and Palestine as the ultimate challenge in deal making.

Asia

While Donald Trump will negotiate hard with China over trade deals and also wants to stand his ground in the disputed South China Sea, he still believes cooperation with China in other political areas is possible and necessary.

In terms of the American military bases in Japan and South Korea, his position seems to be great for starting negotiations versus serving as the result. I believe he will keep US troops in Japan and South Korea although maybe fewer than today, but he wants to get something in return from two of the richest countries in Asia, be it money or infrastructure support in the United States.

Donald Trump brought a refreshing new perspective to the North Korea standoff. Kim Jong-sun is arguably America's biggest threat right now besides ISIS, and by being open to negotiations, the United States could finally address this issue head on. A deal could help the United States be tougher on China on other issues.

Donald Trump will greatly deepen the economic and military ties with India. Economically, India is the new powerhouse for growth, and militarily, India needs the United States to modernize its defense sector. It is under pressure from China's growing footprint in the Indian Ocean. India is ready to commit to the United States in preference over Russia for the first time since the Cold War. The United States also wants to boost India's role in counterbalancing China as well as Iran and Pakistan.

The Southeastern Asian states will continue to be important allies in the world and try to partner even more with a Trump administration to stop China's military expansion in the South China Sea.

Donald Trump realizes that our remaining US military commitments help to secure the gains in Afghanistan that our military and country have given so much for in terms of lives and resources. He will support that and help them to get better infrastructure, which will in return increase the support for the democratic government.

In America's dealing with Pakistan and Iran, I predict he will play hardball. Donald Trump does not believe in the Iran deal, and it will be up to Iranians to prove now the value of the deal for the United States. If they continue with their destructive behavior toward the United States, he will be in a good position to renegotiate the deal or repeal. If Iranian officials are smart and play by the rules and stop some of their most obvious support for terror groups and even partner with the United States on peace in Iraq and Syria and the fight against ISIS, the deal will stand and allow Iran to develop into a real economic power as well.

In terms of Pakistan, there is a lot of opportunity, but first the United States has to gain back respect and self-confidence in dealing with the country. As one of the first steps of his administration, Donald Trump will do everything to get the doctor that helped the United States to find Osama bin Laden out of prison. Continued US-Pakistani cooperation depends on that deal and other Pakistani support against terror rather than

Pakistan officially supporting the United States but unofficially sabotaging efforts. Pakistan is important strategically as it is the only Muslim country with nuclear weapons, but it has played the United States since the raid to capture Osama bin Laden.

Russia

Russia is the most curious case where a Trump presidency could make a big difference from a foreign policy perspective. Vladimir Putin is no democratic, freedom-loving president, but he is a very smart, strategic, and a wildly popular leader in Russia. Russia remains a nuclear superpower, occupies the biggest land mass by far, has vast natural resources, and can influence many countries in the world. Putin is driven by his ego and by a desire to restore dignity and respect for his country in the world to further bolster his popularity in Russia. He knows exactly how far he can go and plays his hand wisely. Invading Crimea was a well-planned and calculated move where he knew that the West was not enough determined to stop it from happening. Donald Trump understands that there is a big opportunity to achieve American foreign policy goals much easier by partnering with Russia, brushing aside ideological concerns. By partnering with Russia, many foreign policy challenges in the Middle East, Asia, and Europe would be much easier to solve. Here are the benefits of such a partnership:

- There would be real peace between the two nuclear superpowers that could destroy the world so many times over, instead of provocative games that could lead to a catastrophe by accident.
- Russia would no longer be inclined to confront the United States militarily on a daily basis to show its strength (daily flyovers over our ships, close to our coasts, etc.).
- The United States and Russia together could solve many of our current crises much faster and share the responsibility (Syria, fight against radical Islam, Pakistan, North Korea, and Iran).

* Both countries would need fewer military resources if working together and trusting each other and could put much more pressure on rogue regimes (Pakistan, Turkey, Iran, and North Korea).
* Europe would be a much safer place without further need to militarize Eastern European NATO states.
* Russia could help more effectively to stop nuclear proliferation to radical terrorist organizations.
* The United States can use Russian boots on the ground, influence, and natural resources and Russia can rely on economic help from the United States, military cooperation, and no more moves that undermine Russian national self-confidence.
* The United States could stop Russia from partnering with China against the United States and therefore be much more effective in slowing China's rise to become a competitive Superpower.

In short, Donald Trump will strengthen and deepen the relations with real and key allies while taking a harder stance on countries and leaders who are not really supporting the United States or are playing America. The benefits and consequences will depend on those countries' cooperation rather than legacy reasons or naïve expectations. This way the United States will again become a more respected, admired, and consistent ally for the right leaders and countries.

It is true that Donald Trump needs to be careful in dealing with strongman Putin and other dictators. He should negotiate with them while not forgetting to push for democracy and freedom rights there. Trump is taking a great approach in ensuring that America continues to stay loyal to those who have helped us tremendously. For example, he is already pushing for the release from Pakistani prison of the Pakistani doctor that tipped off the United States on Osama bin Laden's location. Nobody knows why he is there in the first place, but Trump is pushing for his release even before being elected.

Donald Trump is also promising more common sense in US foreign policy. The Bergdahl prisoner swap, releasing very dangerous Guantanamo detainees that immediately go back to plot to kill more Americans, just does not make sense to anybody. On May 3, 2016 the mastermind behind the attack on the USS *Cole* was released; that attack had cost eleven American lives.

A smart, nonpartisan, non-ideological foreign policy with some fresh ideas and with great negotiators could be something all Americans can agree on.

CHAPTER 4

Trump's Impact and Legacy

———

THE REPUBLICAN PARTY UNDER TRUMP

THE REPUBLICAN PARTY OF 2016 faces a dilemma. On the one hand, it is very successful at the state level as never before, but on the other hand, it has nothing to show for its majority in Congress in terms of results. Nationally Republicans are highly unpopular and appear to be a divided party without an updated agenda or values that are in sync with those of Americans.

The big difference between a populist like Ross Perot in 1992 and Donald Trump in 2016 is that Trump has won the Republican Party nomination, and therefore he has the chance to shape the Republican Party for years to come. (1)

While Trump will influence the Republican Party in a very fundamental and maybe even Reaganesque way if successful, his impact if he is not elected will fade fast, leaving behind a deeply fragmented party that has not modernized and agreed on shared values among its members in a long time. In this case, the lasting impact will be most likely that the Republican Party will amend the primary rules to prevent future populists from making the cut.

Trump's biggest gift to the Republican Party could be his leadership to unite them around a more pragmatic approach to get things done for Americans, centered on an updated agenda and values and a more direct and authentic connection with voters.

US POLITICS AND MEDIA AFTER TRUMP

It is hard to predict how the Trump presidency will go. Sometimes high expectations get crushed, as with Jimmy Carter; in other cases low expectations end in strong presidencies, like Ronald Reagan's. Donald Trump has that anti-ideology, antipartisan feel with adaptability but also a strong drive to get things done, which could serve him well in addition to his excellent negotiation and communication skills. The best thing about his presidency could be a president that is seen as a centrist advocate rather than someone with a biased agenda, bringing Americans together again after their drifting apart from each other ever since the Clinton election in 1992. (2)

In this sense, his impact will be refreshing to democracy: it will be more about personalities and issues and less about ideology and political parties. During Trump's presidency and also after, Americans will no longer be content with two parties blocking each other based on ideology; they will demand even more that issues be pushed through the system by non-ideological leaders, if necessary by populist or direct support from the electorate. Trump has changed for good the way we expect to interact with politicians and what level of authenticity and "realness" we expect from our leaders. Any "political speak," partisan talk, and filtered messaging via the media will be rejected even more.

Whichever political party manages to transition to this new age of politics faster and more wholeheartedly will earn the returns. If the established parties do not manage this transition, more populists will come, new parties will be formed, and social media will create a parallel universe to the current media and to current political leaders. Some of those personalities will use social media effectively to drive topics and initiatives becoming unstoppable even before they reach Congress.

The news media will change as well, and we are already seeing that impact. More people will watch news anchors that do not hold back their personal views but come across as authentic, whether they are at cable news networks, such as Megyn Kelly at Fox News, or on social media channels, such as Tomi Lahren. Those personalities will go their ways independently from partisan news channels. At the same time, the public's opinion will be formed much more by Facebook, Google, Twitter, and Snapchat as the new media outlets. Americans will get news and analysis either directly from reporters on those channels or forwarded by friends and contacts on those channels.

Donald Trump is unique in many ways, and it is hard to imagine how there could be another Trump soon with a similar profile or skillset to win a major political party nomination. He has unique political instinct, impressive salesmanship, and communication skills paired with his wealth, entrepreneurial success, and TV celebrity appeal, plus his unrivaled social media platform leverage and the perfect family backdrop to round it out.

However, there will be more candidates coming that are modern, young, authentic to bring together the new opportunities of "direct democracy" with issues voters really care about and for which they want solutions fast and simple, nationally or locally.

THE IMPACT ON THE WORLD

People from other countries understand that the US president does not reflect the viewpoints of 324 million Americans, who have never been more diverse and more interconnected with the world. It is always so much easier to complain about the wrongdoings of America rather than making the world a better place yourself, especially when you are a rich country but without the will and means to engage militarily for your values. An example of this is ISIS where no nation engages in a ground assault to solve the humanitarian (refugee crisis), human rights (terror regime) but also security (terror attacks) issues.

Donald Trump would most likely significantly improve America's relations with Russia. That in itself would be major progress toward world peace and stability, independent of the opinion someone holds about Putin. Trump will polarize the world more than Obama did, but at the same time, countries will have to do more for America to be seen as a key ally and stay on America's good side. There will be fewer legacy relationships and more real ones. It does not help, for example, that Turkey has always been a key ally of America when its current leader undermines the United States wherever and whenever he can. Trump will look at each international relationship and spread the rewards based on each country's current commitment to America and importance for America. He will not isolate America, as he wants to have key allies in the world that America can rely on.

The world has an inherit bias for Democratic presidents as it sees them as softer spoken and less America-centric than Republican presidents. However, that is not indicative of how those presidents perform in terms of bringing freedom, peace, and human rights to the world. Sometimes well-meaning people cause more harm by being predictable and taken advantage of. Having consistent values and showing a clear willingness to fight for them without publicly taking options of the table could lead to much better results in foreign policy and in getting respect from friends and foes alike.

Today many people in the world are confused about America's foreign policy. America makes peace with Iran although the country sponsors terror and in January 2016 mistreated American sailors and used the video of some of them crying for its own propaganda. Since the US lifted economic sanctions, signed a deal and delivered $400 million in a plane to them in addition to another billion dollar payment they stepped up close encounters with US warships in the Persian gulf. Is the current US administration really hoping that more money will help to make Iran our friend?

Donald Trump as president will not be friendly with everyone or win a Nobel Peace Prize in his second year in office. However, the hope is that America becomes a reliable partner for those who partner with America, and while America will be reluctant to commit forces, it will have a winning and consistent strategy once it engages in international conflict. It will hold other states accountable for their actions and negotiate deals to share the burden of keeping peace in the world. Trump should be the president who gives NATO a new meaning, but only if every member country is willing to commit to contribute its fair share; there should be fewer free riders and more real commitments.

Trump needs to end the chaotic foreign policy of the past eight years. It started with the withdrawal of troops from Iraq, leaving an unstable government. In addition there was no plan for a post-Gadhafi Libya which leads to those countries being vulnerable to ISIS which took over parts of those countries. Obama did not act despite Syria crossing the "red line" he draw and then he underestimated ISIS for the past two years, characterized them as the "JV team". Two years later the ripples from ISIS have caused popular unrest in Europe as shown in right-wing populists gaining power and now UK leaving the EU. This is mainly based on large inflows of predominantly young, male Muslims into those countries without any vetting or control.

Trump should stand up to radical Islamists where they overstep and it leads to trouble or confront China in their game of chicken in the South China Sea. The United States is waging a multiple-year-long air campaign against ISIS without any progress on the ground, while under the world's watch, those modern-day fascists are committing the uttermost cruelties to women and children the world has ever seen. Trump should destroy ISIS as every day ISIS reigns is a shameful day for the world. No more young children, women, or people of all faiths should be killed and tortured in the most appalling ways possible, and this being broadcast around the world. With real leadership, the destruction of ISIS can be accomplished very fast, be it by partnering much better with the Arab states, the Kurds, Turkey, or Russia and willing European countries. ISIS is a bigger problem for Europe and Russia, so they have clear incentives to engage. ISIS has already survived for two years, the longer it does the more it will be perceived as defying the West and the winner image will create a bigger following which will in turn lead to more terrorist bombings like in Orlando or Istanbul in June 2016.

EUROPE

For many Europeans, Donald Trump embodies what they love to hate about America. He is compared in European newspapers to their own nationalist leaders. In a German newspaper, he was compared to a former rock star in that country, Dieter Bohlen, as both of them are famous for being "loudmouths" and insulting people. This politics-as-entertainment style is something that Europe does not have yet.

Europe is at its crossroads, with or without a US president called Donald Trump, as the Brexit referendum result shows. Trump as US president will help Europe to either partner much better with America or see the need for stronger self-reliance and a real unification of the continent, especially when it comes to foreign policy and military cooperation. After the UK will exit the EU, there will be an even closer relationship between the UK and the US militarily and economically. At the same time the EU gets another chance to reform itself with fewer countries however also with reduced economic and military power.

Europe is a great, diverse, and prosperous continent with a lot of unused potential. Unfortunately, the EU has proven to be unwilling or unable to do anything more than provide a common market despite a big bureaucracy and many resources invested in its political aspirations. If the EU were to adopt a common foreign policy and military strategy it could become a real and positive superpower for peace and human rights in the world. Unfortunately, EU institutions are still undemocratic, and the EU itself is stuck halfway in a highly unsatisfactory and inefficient stage between being a union of strong national states and a real integrated "United States of Europe." The EU is rich and wields power in international trade relations but is not capable to defeating ISIS, securing its border, progressing human and women's rights internationally (e.g., in Turkey and Syria), or defending itself. The current migrant crisis and blackmailing by Turkey reveals the dilemma blatantly. The most powerful economic power in the world is unable to secure its borders and risks being overrun by the biggest migration wave from outside Europe since centuries, and all because it is unable to deal with a group of thirty thousand thugs in Syria calling itself ISIS. Because of this foreign policy weakness, it has to keep pandering to a quasi-dictator-led Turkey to keep millions of refugees and thousands of terrorists out of the EU. At the same time, hundreds of refugees are dying in the Mediterranean Sea every week trying to cross over from Africa or the Middle East, turning it into an appalling graveyard of humanity. If the EU wants to survive as a political institution, it has to act fast and decisive to do the following:

* Secure its outer borders by all means and independent of Turkey. That means stopping the boats before they start in Africa and Turkey to prevent more suffering. Anything else will overburden European populations and drive nationalists to power that will paralyze the EU even more.
* Build up a common foreign policy and military infrastructure. As a first step, such a multilateral force could create a safe zone in Syria for all refugees and fight back ISIS. This would make Europe strong, solve the refugee crisis, prevent attacks such as in Paris, Brussels or Nice and be a big step forward for humanity.
* Create a democratic structure for EU leadership with a president and four to five ministers that the EU population will vote for directly on the same day every four or five years. Enable the European parliament to build a real government for Europe with democratic controls.

If the EU does not take these next steps soon, it will fall victim to nationalists in the individual states that will call for their nations' exit or undermine any common effort and the EU institutions itself. The rise of nationalists is driven by the incompetence and inability of the EU to act on destroying ISIS, securing the border, stopping terrorism, and improving economic growth and opportunities for so many Europeans.

The impact of the refugee crisis was unevenly spread across EU states. In many European countries (especially Sweden, Germany, and Austria), the high influx of young Muslim men from Syria has led to an uneven male-female ratio among fifteen- to thirty-year-olds. Because of this influx, different cultural and religious norms, and other factors, there have been more social unrest, anti-Semitism, sexual violence against women and children, and general feeling of less security, leading to the surge of right-wing populist nationalists in many countries. In addition there is the threat of terrorists either being let in or being able to recruit frustrated young Muslim men as recent attacks in Bavaria have shown.

Europe needs a new vision for its future and a cross-country popu-list movement that drives those institutional reforms forward to create one united Europe, at least for foreign policy and militarily, especially if President Trump declares that the United States is no longer willing to pay 70% of the bill for the collective security.

> Europe's refugee crisis has led to a rise in the number of Trump-style right-wing populists. The forces driving those movements are the same across Europe: large-scale immigration of Muslim men, disillusion-ment with the economic results of globalization and free trade, fear of terrorism, and cynicism about career politicians. In France, Marine Le Pen has a change to become the next president, Geert Wilders is popu-lar in the Netherlands, and even Germany has a nationalist movement now as Angela Merkel has moved to the left. In Poland and Hungary, meanwhile, two avowedly nationalistic governments are continuing to strengthen their grips on power. Viktor Orban is the Donald Trump of Hungary, a self-styled strongman who has gone ahead and built fences on its borders with Austria, Croatia, Serbia, Slovenia, and Romania. Poland and Slovakia have also refused to take in Syrian refugees de-spite previously committing to the EU. (3)

The Brexit vote is the blueprint of a global phenomenon happening right now. It's a people defying the warnings of their government, cultural icons and business leaders. It is based on the same frustration, insecurity and alienation that is driving voters to elect more populist and nationalist candidates across Europe. The backbone of democracy, the middle class, feels less and less rep-resented by their traditional politicians as they feel squeezed between a global elite getting insanely rich while evading taxes and poor people or recent immigrants getting most of the government benefits they have to pay for with their taxes. This sentiment is fueled by economic insecurity driven by globalization and the technological revolution. At the same time those mainly white and male voters see an elite-driven disdain for the idea of a nation having a right to pick their immigrants and having the obligation to put their people first. They feel that their concerns are regarded as racism and frowned upon. While the EU has delivered a common currency and eased travel of goods, money and people between countries it has never provided a sense of togetherness among European people or messaged a united vision or shared set of values in a meaningful way to its over 500 million people (before Brexit).

Millions of Europeans cheer and enjoy the European song contest each year where they can vote for the best song among European nations but the EU has not yet been able to establish the democratic election of any EU leadership position in a direct and democratic vote where all Europeans can vote on the same day across all nations. A direct vote for a policy or an EU politician across member states on the same day would create a much stronger feeling of common destiny, transparency and connectedness. Especially young people across Europe are hoping for that vision, unity and reform within the EU.

Mexico

The big question is how the Trump presidency will impact Mexico and its relationship with the United States. Former Mexican president Vincente Fox and many top government officials have already weighed in on that. The current Mexican president Enrique Nieto has already changed the embassy team in Washington, DC, to prepare for a Trump presidency. Twenty-six consulates in the United States have changed leadership already. The border wall will impact Mexico in many unpredictable ways, but some could be good for Mexico. It will disrupt the drug cartels and make it easier for Mexican law enforcement along the border to go after criminals and drug dealers. The cartels will find new ways to transport drugs, but it will be costlier, and their couriers and systems will be more vulnerable. This could lead not only to fewer people in the United States consuming drugs owing to higher prices but also to fewer escape routes for Mexican criminals. As routes back to the United States are blocked and more illegals are deported to Mexico, more people will try to come to America legally. If wages in the US will increase based on less competition from illegal workers the legal Mexicans in the US will earn higher wages and be able to send more money back to their relatives in Mexico.

Asia

Donald Trump's announcement that South Korea and Japan should take care of their own self-defense shocked Japan and South Korea. Without US guarantees, countries such as Japan would have to build up their militaries dramatically, causing a new arms race in Asia. In addition, China might feel inclined to take over Taiwan if it believes that America is no longer willing to defend Taiwan.

However, leaders in Asia should not be panicking, as those positions on foreign policy in Asia are among those Trump would give up as president, based on geopolitical strategy and after being advised by military generals. Retreating from those bases and treaties with ASEAN countries uniting against China would mean willfully ceding US global leadership and handing more power to China. Donald Trump will realize that whoever takes the Chinese challenge to America's dominance serious—and he does—needs strong allies and resources in the region.

China is currently on a dangerous course if not confronted by the United States. It is getting cocky with American military in the region and provoking its Asian neighbors more and more. It now sends warships to Japanese seas and has upgraded its military installations in the South China Sea. The United States needs to counter China's activities on the seas, in cyberspace, and in the region's airspace.

The only question is how and when Donald Trump will reverse course on his statements. It might be in the general election campaign, or after meeting with his Japanese and South Korean counterparts for the first time, or while preparing to take over the presidency and talking to his military advisers.

WHY POPULISTS CAN BE A GIFT FOR DEMOCRACIES

Many people see populists as something negative, especially as they see them close to either communism or fascism. Populists have been around since there was democracy, and also in the United States on both sides of the political spectrum. They fulfill an important function in any democracy as they refresh the parliament or Congress as well as political parties. They bring in new voters and disenfranchised people who would otherwise not engage in democratic elections and the political process.

Strongmen have always been a part of politics, from Greek democracy all the way to modern elections, as ambitious individuals shake up their nations. They come to power democratically right now, driven by public dissatisfaction and the collapse of the center based on fears of terrorism, uncontrolled immigration, and the economic decline of the middle class.

> *Wikipedia* defines populism as the political philosophy and movement around it that is supporting the rights and power of the people in their struggles against the privileged elite. (4)

In today's world, populism is driven by the economic decline of the middle class based on globalization and technological revolution, and a sense of loss of sovereignty paired with the fear of no longer being heard by politicians. National populists can divide societies, damage relations between states and in the worst case, lead to less individual freedom up to dictatorship, though only in underdeveloped democracies like Turkey.

Here are ten ways in which populists in mature democracies can have a positive impact on democracy:

- They stoke interest and involvement in politics
- They create more civic consciousness as even people from normally less-engaged demographics, such as young people, see that some of the proposals could impact their lives and the lives of others.
- People engage in politics more holistically, not just with their brains but also with their emotions. Populists force other politicians to become more empathetic to the concerns and topics of voters they previously neglected on a purely rational basis.
- Disenfranchised citizens who never felt that any traditional politician cared about them get motivated to engage.
- More legal immigrants get naturalized as they now have a motivation to have their voices heard, increasing national unity.
- People feeling frustrated and angry with politics have an outlet for their anger and frustration that can be used productively and in democratic process. In some cases, those voices and people would otherwise have been captured by more extreme groups outside of the democratic process or would have resorted to violent means.
- Populism leads to more diversity of opinions in the political arena rather than just mainstream opinions being heard, and there are fewer taboos around some topics (e.g., illegal immigration or the negative side of international trade).
- More people directly engage with populists on social media or at rallies as they feel a stronger connection to populists; they feel somebody cares about them at last.
- They help to remove the bias in the news media as news outlets have to report what they are saying in order to get ratings, help to simplify the language, and prevent politicians from hiding behind complex language and formalities.

* They bring together in their defense people who would otherwise never join forces, which can be a unifier for a country in both directions.

Populists will thrive as long as the middle class feels under pressure and/ or is shrinking. Commonsense politics, economic opportunity, a strong political vision, and real help for middle-class topics can reduce populism.

It is interesting that populism in the United States has so far been more associated with the left and in Europe more with the right. It is because in Europe, populists on the left were called socialists, something less known in the United States before the 2016 election and Bernie Sanders. The United States has actually a long history of populist movements. Just before the Trump and Sanders campaign were the Occupy Wall Street and Tea Party populist movements. In that sense, Trump and Sanders follow those populist campaigns. The first populist movement in the United States was the Populist Party of the 1890s. Farmers and labor unions denounced an economic system that served the few at the cost of the many. Other early populist political parties in the United States included the Greenback Party, the Progressive Party of 1912 led by Theodore Roosevelt, the Progressive Party of 1924 led by Robert M. La Follette Sr., and the Share Our Wealth movement of Huey Long in 1933–35. Former governor of Alabama George Wallace led a populist movement that carried five states and won 13.5% of the popular vote in the 1968 presidential election. In the 1992 and 1996 elections, populists such as Pat Buchanan and Ross Perot had some success and later Ralph Nader on the left. The Tea Party movement used populist rhetoric, large outdoor rallies, populist rhetoric, and the use of patriotic symbols (notably the Don't Tread on Me Gadsden flag) in the tradition of the antifederalist movement of the 1780s. The Occupy movement had the slogan "We are the 99%" going against the wealthiest 1% and was the first major populist movement on the US left since the 1930s. (4)

THE END OF THE BUSH AND CLINTON DYNASTIES

Dynasties fail when they lose touch with the electorate. This was as true for ancient kings as it is for modern presidential dynasties in the most powerful country in the world. Donald Trump could be the person to effectively end not only the Bush dynasty but also the Clinton political dynasty in November.

The Clinton dynasty on the Democratic side and the Bush dynasty on the Republican side have been impressive and the most powerful dynasties since the conclusion of World War II in the US. While the Kennedys had only three years of presidential power, the Clintons already have eight on their books, and it could become as much as sixteen years. Plus they have been dominating Democratic Party politics and administrations for a total of twenty-four years.

Even more impressive is the Bush dynasty. They already had two presidents and one vice president for a total of twelve years of presidential power and twenty years as president or vice president of the United States, plus a governorship in Texas and Florida. Jeb Bush was the favorite for this year's election but was stopped cold by Donald Trump very early. It is no surprise that the Bush family has stated that they will remain on the sidelines in this election as they cannot and will not support the Republican nominee—Trump has kept the Bush family from setting a new record in presidential power grabbing by one family.

It is outright astounding to see two political families hold so much control over the most powerful country in the world, a democracy of 324 million people, for such a long time. Combined, those two dynasties have already had three presidents, one vice president, three governors (Texas, Florida, Arkansas), and a combined twenty years as US president and has played key roles in US politics and both major parties for thirty-six years, from 1980 until 2016—and that is if Hillary Clinton loses her run.

If Clinton were to win the presidency, the United States would be looking at four presidents and twenty-four to twenty-eight years of presidents in only two political families. This is what American political dynasties look like. Ironically, if Donald Trump becomes the forty-fifth US president, he could not only end the Bush and Clinton dynasties' grip on the presidency but also signal that America is ready for more diversity among its presidents and presidential candidates.

Afterword

ENJOY THE PROCESS TO ELECT our forty-fifth president; be open to new, disruptive ideas and fresh thinking how to organize government and bridge the partisan divide and keep us safe. We vote for our kids and for generations to come, and also for the leader of the free world. Without America, this planet would be a far more dangerous place; just look at what is happening in Syria when America is not fully engaged.

It is the time when our great country, home to over 324 million Americans, has to elect one man or woman to lead us all. We are the most diverse people the world has ever known, all religions, races, backgrounds, and attitudes in one country, competing for wealth, jobs, schools, and opportunities for our kids every day. But despite all our differences, we come together in this democratic process to make a popular choice of who should lead us, govern us, and represent us all.

Let's put all our trust in the American people and the democratic institutions that have served us so well for 240 years. We, all together as Americans, have collectively made smart choices in the past and will continue to do so now. Maybe the best single feature of the American presidential system is its term limit, which helps to overcome people's preference for stability and the known over the unknown and taking risks. Every eight years, Americans are forced to take risks and let somebody new bring in his or her ideas. This rattles the system, refreshes government, and makes our country better.

There is no place like America in the world. It has to continue to be the shining city on the hill, the beacon of freedom for generations worldwide to come. Who can ever replace or replicate our success, our beautiful country between two oceans, the innovative and adaptive people, the multicultural melting pot and our dynamism? What other country can transform migrants into proud citizens that feel truly at home so fast and so completely? And what other country is so selfless that it not only stopped two world wars fought on a different continent but also has its most wealthy people join forces and pledge most of their wealth to eradicate the world of illnesses, poverty, and war forever?

At a personal level, this book has been a great way for me to channel my enormous interest in US politics and democracy. I love discussing politics, ideas to improve our country, and the trends impacting our media, politics, and society. I hope that this election will help America to overcome the biggest issues in my opinion: the paralyzing partisanship, shrinking middle class and missing leadership in foreign policy.

I'm so excited about being able to vote for the first time.

I would enjoy discussing with as many readers as possible and getting your feedback, opinions, and ideas. Please check out my website www.the-united-states-of-trump.com, or follow me on Twitter @theusoftrump

Acknowledgments

———

A BOOK IS A JOURNEY, and this one has been a very inspiring and exciting one. I learned a lot about publishing, about writing, and about myself. While many have questioned why I would write a book about Donald Trump, I was always sure this book needed to be written. His personality and the status of American politics, society, and media after eight years of Obama's "hope and change" presidency afforded a deeper look at America, the trends, issues and the mood of the electorate. I wanted to explain more about the primaries but also look at the general election and what lies ahead. Many great books have been written about Trump but this one solely focuses on him as a politician.

Thanks so much to my wife, Martina, for being tolerant with my nightly sessions powered by caffeine and the sheer desire to write this book. You are the rock and the soul of our amazing and joyous family. Vincent and Benjamin, my two young sons, thanks for reminding me every day about the beauty of life and helping me to grow as a father and human being and inspiring me to fight for a better world for all children.

Steve thanks so much for your inspiration and discussions, and for cheering me up along this journey. Thank you, John and Patsy, Karl and Lisa, for not only being such great neighbors but also providing such valuable feedback on this book. I'm eternal grateful that my parents, Heidi and Peter, always promoted political discussions at our home and encouraged me to form my own opinions and get involved in politics at a very young age. The team at CreateSpace was great in bringing this book to life and made this journey a very enjoyable and smooth ride, thanks a lot.

NOTES

Chapter 1: The Trump Phenomenon Explained

(1) Sherman, Gabriel, "Inside the most unorthodox campaign in political history," *New York Magazine*, Apr. 4–17, 2016, pp. 33–37, 93–95

(2) Milbank, Dana, "Americans' optimism is dying," *Washington Post*, Aug. 12, 2014, https://www.washingtonpost.com/opinions/dana-milbank-americans-optimism-is-dying/2014/08/12/f81808d8-224c-11e4-8593-da634b334390_story.html

(3) "Fear trumps hope," *Economist*, May 7, 2016, pp. 20–22

(4) Packer, George, "Head of class," *New Yorker*, May 16, 2016, http://www.newyorker.com/magazine/2016/05/16/how-donald-trump-appeals-to-the-white-working-class

(5) Murray, Charles, "Trump's America," *Wall Street Journal*, Feb. 12, 2016, http://www.wsj.com/articles/donald-trumps-america-1455290458

(6) Rasmussen Reports, "Congressional performance," Feb. 22, 2016, http://www.rasmussenreports.com/public_content/politics/mood_of_america/congressional_performance

(7) Pew Research Center, "GOP's favorability rating edges lower," *People Press*, Apr. 28, 2016, http://www.people-press.org/2016/04/28/gops-favorability-rating-edges-lower/

(8) Spiliakos, Pete, "Donald Trump and the revenge of the scorned," Jan. 7, 2016, http://www.firstthings.com/web-exclusives/2016/01/donald-trump-and-the-revenge-of-the-scorned?gclid=Cj0KEQj w6Ya5BRDdyOewyo_Z_64BEiQA-fVKe_meiejTSnC8a9Eh-ZoASm5wnZ9il5x82Tfg0YRxpVooaAtxo8P8HAQ

(9) Seib, Gerald F., "The Tea Party eyes Donald Trump warily," *Wall Street Journal*, May 16, 2016, http://www.wsj.com/articles/the-tea-party-eyes-donald-trumpwarily-1463411463

(10) D'Antonio, Michael, *Never enough*, 2015, Thomas Dunne Books, St. Martin's Press, p. 217

(11) Sherman, Gabriel, "Inside the most unorthodox campaign in political history," *New York Magazine*, Apr. 4–17, 2016, pp. 33–37, 93–95

(12) D'Antonio, Michael, *Never enough*, 2015, Thomas Dunne Books, St. Martin's Press, pp. 2-4

(13) "Megyn Kelly presents", aired on May 17 on Fox, http://www.fox.com/megyn-kelly-presents/article/fox-news-channel-anchor-megyn-kelly%E2%80%99s-first-primetime-fox-broadcasting-special-%E2%80%9Cmegyn-kelly

(14) Jordan, Mary and O'Connell, Jonathan, "Ivanka Trump: The 'Anti-Donald' works to protect the billion-dollar brand," *Washington Post*, Mar. 28, 2016, https://www.washingtonpost.com/politics/ivanka-trump-the-anti-donald-works-to-protect-the-billion-dollar-brand/2016/03/27/49613d2c-cb48-11e5-a7b2-5a2f824b02c9_story.html

(15) Confessore, Nicholas and Yourish, Karen, "Measuring Donald Trump's mammoth advantage in free media", *New York Times*, The Upshot, Mar. 15, 2016 ; http://www.nytimes.com/2016/03/16/upshot/measuring-donald-trumps-mammoth-advantage-in-free-media.html

(16) Ellefson, Lindsey, "CBS CEO on Trump Campaign: It 'May Not be Good for America, but It's Damn Good for CBS", Feb. 29, 2016, http://www.mediaite.com/online/cbs-ceo-on-trump-campaign-it-may-not-be-good-for-america-but-its-damn-good-for-cbs/

(17) "Jon Stewart being interviewed by David Axelrod in front of students," *Huffington Post*, May 9, 2016, University of Chicago, Institute of Politics, http://m.huffpost.com/us/entry/jon-stewart-donald-trump-man-baby_us_57313296e4b016f37896d670

(18) Cuban, Mark, "Some thoughts on the presidential race and sociocapitalism", *blogmaverick.com*, Feb. 8, 2016, http://blogmaverick.com/2016/02/08/some-thoughts-on-the-presidential-race-and-sociocapitalism/

(19) "Fear trumps hope," *Economist*, May 7–13, 2016, pp. 20–22

(20) "Donald Trump's announcement speech," *Time* staff, June 16, 2015, http://time.com/3923128/donald-trump-announcement-speech/d

(21) D'Antonio, Michael, *Never enough*, 2015, Thomas Dunne Books, St. Martin's Press, p. 64

(22) Trump, Donald J., *Crippled America: How to make America great again*, 2015, Simon & Schuster, p. 11

(23) D'Antonio, Michael, *Never enough*, 2015, Thomas Dunne Books, St. Martin's Press, p. 211

(24) Cuban, Mark, "Some thoughts on the presidential race and sociocapitalism", blogmaverick.com, Feb. 8, 2016, http://blogmaverick.com/2016/02/08/some-thoughts-on-the-presidential-race-and-sociocapitalism/

(25) Trout, Jack and Ries, Al, *The 22 immutable laws of marketing*, HarperBusiness, 1994; Ries, Al and Laura Ries, *The 22 immutable laws of branding*, HarperBusiness, ries.com, 1998

(26) Thompson, Derek, "Who are Donald Trump's supporters, really?," *Atlantic*, Mar. 1, 2016, http://www.theatlantic.com/politics/archive/2016/03/who-are-donald-trumps-supporters-really/471714/

(27) Sherman, Gabriel, "Inside the most unorthodox campaign in political history," *New York Magazine*, Apr. 4–17, 2016, pp. 33–37, 93–95, Print version, http://nymag.com/daily/intelligencer/2016/04/inside-the-donald-trump-presidential-campaign.html

(28) Gobry, Pascal-Emmanuel, "Why Donald Trump is the political equivalent of a Silicon Valley startup," *Week*, May 26, 2016, http://theweek.com/articles/626366/why-donald-trump-political-equivalent-silicon-valley-startup

(29) D'Antonio, Michael, *Never enough*, 2015, Thomas Dunne Books, St. Martin's Press, p. 11

(30) D'Antonio, Michael, *Never enough*, 2015, Thomas Dunne Books, St. Martin's Press, p. 59

(31) Puschak, Evan, "How Donald Trump answers a question", https://www.youtube.com/watch?v=_aFo_BV-UzI&feature=youtu.be, Dec. 30, 2015, http://www.patreon.com/nerdwriterf

(32) Romano, Andrew, "The strange power of Donald Trump's speech patterns," *Yahoo*, Mar. 31, 2016, https://www.yahoo.com/news/the-strange-power-of-donald-1397103083307062.htmld

(33) Liberatore, Stacy, "Donald Trump's language could win him the presidency: Candidates that use emotional words get more votes in times of crisis," *Daily Mail*, Mar. 21, 2016, http://www.dailymail.co.uk/sciencetech/article-3502925/Donald-Trump-s-language-win-presidency-Candidates-use-emotional-words-votes-times-crisis.html

(34) Smith, Allison Jane, "Donald Trump speaks like a sixth-grader. All politicians should," *Washington Post*, May 3, 2016, https://www.washingtonpost.com/posteverything/wp/2016/05/03/donald-trump-speaks-like-a-sixth-grader-all-politicians-should/

(35) Miller, Claire, "Measuring Trump's language: Bluster but also words that appeal to women," *Upshot*, Mar. 14, 2016, http://www.nytimes.com/2016/03/15/upshot/donald-trump-is-among-the-most-feminine-sounding-candidates.html?_r=0h

(36) Harbeck, James, "How Donald Trump hypnotized America," *Week*, May 17, 2016, http://theweek.com/articles/623396/how-donald-trump-hypnotized-america

(37) Romano, Andrew, "The strange power of Donald Trump's speech patterns," *Yahoo*, Mar. 31, 2016, https://www.yahoo.com/news/the-strange-power-of-donald-1397103083307062.htmld

(38) Razavi, Katrina, "The science behind Donald Trump's body language," *Huffington Post*, May 10, 2016, http://www.huffingtonpost.com/katrina-razavi/the-science-behind-donald-trump-body-language_b_9865432.htmld

(39) Atkin, Emily, "What language experts find so strange about Donald Trump," *ThinkProgress*, Sep. 15, 2015, http://thinkprogress.org/politics/2015/09/15/3701215/donald-trump-talks-funny-2/

(40) Beckel, Michael, "Donald Trump steamrolling toward nomination despite negative ad blitz," Center for Public Integrity, Apr. 27, 2016, https://

www.publicintegrity.org/2016/04/27/19597/donald-trump-steam-rolling-toward-nomination-despite-negative-ad-blitz

(41) Schaeffer, Adam B., "How anti-Trump ads could win Trump the nom-ination," *Politico*, Apr. 9, 2016, http://www.politico.com/magazine/story/2016/04/anti-trump-ads-backfire-213819#ixzz49SptI3eX

(42) "The Art of the Steal," Time, Time staff, print version, Jan. 7, 2016, pp. 34–39, http://www.donaldjtrump.com/media/donald-trumps-art-of-the-steal

(43) Westfall, Sandra Sobieraj and Triggs, Charlotte, "Who is the real Donald Trump?," *People*, Apr. 11, 2016, http://www.people.com/article/real-donald-trump-people-special-report

(44) Puschak, Evan, "Why Donald Trump is a gift to democracy", The Nerdwriter1, Sep. 23, 2015, https://www.youtube.com/watch?v=9Tji1g0WrPw; http://www.patreon.com/nerdwriter

(45) "The rise of a rule breaker," Time staff, *Time*, pages 6-7, May 2016, special edition

(46) Collins, Eliza, "Les Moonves: Trump's run is damn good for CBS", Politico, Feb. 29, 2016, http://www.politico.com/blogs/on-media/2016/02/les-moonves-trump-cbs-220001

(47) Zelizer, Julian, "Why Trump is the next Walter White," CNN, May 30, 2016, http://www.cnn.com/2016/05/30/opinions/trump-as-tv-anti-hero-julian-zelizer/

(48) Thoma, Mark, "Populism vs. nationalism," *Economist*, Nov. 8, 2006, http://economistsview.typepad.com/economistsview/2006/11/populism_vs_nat.html

(49) Keith, Tamara, "5 ways Bernie Sanders and Donald Trump are more alike than you think," NPR, Feb. 8, 2016, http://www.npr.org/2016/02/08/465974199/what-do-sanders-and-trump-have-in-common-more-than-you-think

(50) Galston, William, "Americans are in no mood for a Trump presiden-cy," *Newsweek*, Apr. 8, 2016, http://www.newsweek.com/americans-no-mood-trump-presidency-445590

CHAPTER 2: CLINTON VS. TRUMP

(1)   Balz, Dan and Clement, Scott, "2016 election shapes up as a contest of negatives," *Washington Post*, May 21, 2016, https://www.washingtonpost.com/politics/poll-election-2016-shapes-up-as-a-contest-of-negatives/2016/05/21/8d4ccfd6-1ed3-11e6-b6e0-c53b7ef63b45_story.html

(2)   Blanton, Dana, "Trump tops Clinton, both seem as deeply flawed candidates," Fox News App, May 18, 2016, http://www.foxnews.com/politics/2016/05/18/fox-news-poll-trump-tops-clinton-both-seen-as-deeply-flawed-candidates.html

(3)   Wikipedia – Shooting of Kathryn Steinle, https://en.wikipedia.org/wiki/Shooting_of_Kathryn_Steinle

(4)   Rogers, Ed, "The long lines at airports are a problem for Hillary Clinton," *Washington Post*, May 25, 2016, https://www.washingtonpost.com/blogs/post-partisan/wp/2016/05/25/the-long-lines-at-airports-are-a-problem-for-hillary-clinton/

(5)   Website to predict electorate college, http://www.270towin.com/

(6)   Balz, Dan, "How Trump vs. Clinton could reshape the electoral map," *Washington Post*, Mar. 19, 2016, https://www.washingtonpost.com/politics/how-trump-vs-clinton-would-reshape-the-electoral-map/2016/03/19/783a834c-ed35-11e5-b0fd-073d5930a7b7_story.html

(7)   Bernstein, David S., "Donald Trump can actually win if Clinton makes these four mistakes. Spoiler alert: She's already making all of them," *Politico*, May 27, 2016, http://www.politico.com/magazine/story/2016/05/2016-election-hillary-clinton-campaign-loses-defeated-donald-trump-213924

(8)   Beckwith, Ryan Teague, "Read Donald Trump's speech on the Orlando shooting", *Time.com*, online, Jun. 13, 2016, http://time.com/4367120/orlando-shooting-donald-trump-transcript/

(9)   Starr, Barbara, "CIA director grave warning: ISIS as dangerous as ever", cnn.*com*, Online, June 20, 2016, http://www.cnn.com/2016/06/16/politics/john-brennan-cia-isis/

(10)   Browne, Ryan, "Top general: U.S. strategy against ISIS in Libya makes no sense", *cnn.com,* Online, June 22, 2016, http://www.cnn.com/2016/06/21/politics/general-no-strategy-isis-libya/

(11)   Goins-Philip, Tre, "The USA must act: Former Islamic state sex slave tells Congress the group must be 'terminated'", TheBlaze.com, Online, Jun. 21, 2016, http://www.theblaze.com/stories/2016/06/21/the-usa-must-act-former-islamic-state-sex-slave-tells-congress-the-terror-group-must-be-terminated/

(12)   Besheer, Mohamed, "A new estimate of the U.S. Muslim population", *Pew Research Center*, Jan. 6, 2016, http://www.pewresearch.org/fact-tank/2016/01/06/a-new-estimate-of-the-u-s-muslim-population/

(13)   Kephart, Janice, "Immigration and Terrorism", Sep. 2005, CIS.org, http://cis.org/articles/2005/kephart.html

(14)   Boyle, Matthew, "Senate Committee: 580 Terror Convictions in U.S. Since 9/11, 380 Terrorists Are Foreign-Born", Jun. 22, 2016, Breitbart.com, Online, http://www.breitbart.com/big-government/2016/06/22/senate-committee-580-terror-convictions-in-u-s-since-911-380-terrorists-are-foreign-born/

(15)   Ulanoff, Lance, "It's official: Most of us get our news now from social media," *Mashable*, May 27, 2016, http://mashable.com/2016/05/26/pew-news-social-media-study/#mpQxW8v58gqZ

(16)   Blanchard, Lauren, "Johnson wins libertarian party presidential nomination", Online, May 29, 2016, http://www.foxnews.com/politics/2016/05/29/johnson-wins-libertarian-party-presidential-nomination.htmlFox News App, May 27, 2016

(17)   "Republican Party favorability tracking poll", Pew Research Center, June 28, 2016, http://www.pewresearch.org/data-trend/political-attitudes/republican-party-favorability/

(18) "United States presidential approval rating", Wikipedia, June 28, 2016, https://en.wikipedia.org/wiki/United_States_presidential_approval_rating

(19) Halper, Evan, "Be nice to Hillary Clinton online – or risk a confrontation with her super PAC", L.A. Times, May 9, 2016, Online, http://www.latimes.com/politics/la-na-clinton-digital-trolling-20160506-snap-htmlstory.html

(20) Thomas, Shawna, "Hillary Clinton questions Trump's level of success," NBC News, May 22, 2016, http://www.nbcnews.com/meet-the-press/hillary-clinton-questions-trump-s-level-success-n578246

(21) Scher, Brent, "Hillary Clinton has spent three times more on primary than Donald Trump," *Washington Free Beacon*, June 1, 2016, http://freebeacon.com/politics/hillary-clinton-spent-three-times-money-primary-donald-trump/

(22) Reston, Laura, "Can Democratic attack ads tear down Donald Trump?," *New Republic*, Mar. 25, 2016, https://newrepublic.com/article/131996/can-democratic-attack-ads-tear-donald-trump

(23) Beckwith, Ryan Teague, "Read Donald Trump's Speech Criticizing Hillary Clinton on Foreign Policy", June 22, 2016, time.com Online, http://time.com/4378270/donald-trump-hillary-clinton-foreign-policy-speech-transcript/

(24) Foran, Clare, "Making the case against Donald Trump," *Atlantic*, May 19, 2016, http://www.theatlantic.com/politics/archive/2016/05/donald-trump-attack-ads/483560/

(25) Video of Trump speech at NRA convention on May, 20, 2016, https://www.youtube.com/watch?v=zGnf0x6FJY8

(26) Kurtzleben, Danielle, "The Trump-Clinton gender gap could be the largest in 60 years," NPR, May 26, 2016, http://www.npr.org/2016/05/26/479319725/the-trump-clinton-gender-gap-could-be-the-largest-in-more-than-60-years

(27) Dann, Carrie, "Six numbers that show why Clinton is still the favorite in 2016," NBC News, May 28, 2016, http://www.nbcnews.com/politics/2016-election/six-numbers-show-why-clinton-still-favorite-2016-n581691

(28)   Concha, Joe, "Online polls now firmly on Trump's side as candidate masterfully adopts Hillary's greatest strength," Mediaite, May 19, 2016, http://www.mediaite.com/online/polls-now-firmly-on-trumps-side-as-candidate-masterfully-adopts-hillarys-greatest-strength/

(29)   Goldberg, Michelle, "Trump's speech about Hillary was terrifyingly effective", *Slate,* Online, June 22, 2016, http://www.slate.com/articles/news_and_politics/politics/2016/06/donald_trump_s_speech_about_hillary_clinton_was_terrifyingly_effective.html

(30)   Beinart, Peter, "The real scandal of Hillary Clinton's e-mails," *Atlantic,* May 27, 2016, http://www.theatlantic.com/politics/archive/2016/05/e-mail-hillary-clinton/484634/

(31)   "Judge Napolitano's chamber," Video by Andrew Napolitano, Fox News, May 12, 2016, http://video.foxnews.com/v/4890754150001/napolitano-hillary-clintons-no-good-very-bad-week/?#sp=show-clips

(32)   Johnson, Alex, "What the State Department e-mail report means for Hillary Clinton," NBC News, May 26, 2016, http://www.nbcnews.com/news/us-news/what-state-department-e-mail-report-means-hillary-clinton-n580516

(33)   Hoft, Jim, "Trump in Spokane: Hillary Clinton hurt many women, the women Bill abused", thegatewaypundit.com, May 7, 2016, http://www.thegatewaypundit.com/2016/05/trump-spokane-hillary-clinton-hurt-many-women-women-bill-abused-video/

(34)   "Trump refers to alleged Bill Clinton sexual indiscretions as rape", Foxnews, Online, May 19, 2016, http://www.foxnews.com/politics/2016/05/19/trump-refers-to-alleged-bill-clinton-sexual-indiscretions-as-rape.html

(35)   Gass, Nick, "Donald Trump mentions rape discussing Bill Clinton," *Politico,* May 18, 2016, http://www.politico.com/story/2016/05/donald-trump-mentions-rape-discussing-bill-clinton-223348#ixzz496EFcqlC

(36)   Zimmermann, Malia, "Flight logs show Bill Clinton flew on sex offenders jet much more than previously known," *Fox News,* May 13, 2016,

http://www.foxnews.com/us/2016/05/13/flight-logs-show-bill-clinton-flew-on-sex-offenders-jet-much-more-than-previously-known.html

(37) Canning, Ernest, "The Clintons and the sordid UBS affair," *The Hill*, Mar. 10, 2016, http://thehill.com/blogs/congress-blog/presidential-campaign/272396-the-clintons-and-the-sordid-ubs-affair

(38) Sirota, David and Perez, Andrew, "Clinton Foundation owners got weapons deals from Hillary Clinton's State Department," *IBTimes*, May 26, 2016, http://www.ibtimes.com/clinton-foundation-donors-got-weapons-deals-hillary-clintons-state-department-1934187

(39) Pollock, Richard, "Pay Gap Alert: Clinton Foundation Male Execs Earn 38% More Than Women", thedailycaller.com, Online, April 12, 2016, http://dailycaller.com/2016/04/12/pay-gap-alert-clinton-foundation-male-execs-earn-38-more-than-women/#ixzz4CuRaXh99

(40) McAfee, Tierney, "Bernie or bust: Why 20% of Sanders supporters say they would vote for Donald Trump over Hillary Clinton," *People*, May 23, 2016, http://www.people.com/article/bernieorbust-sanders-supporters-vote-trump-clinton

(41) Tooley, Heather, "Megyn Kelly thinks Donald Trump can move women in his favor?", starpulse.com, Online, May 3, 2016, http://www.starpulse.com/megyn-kelly-thinks-donald-trump-can-move-women-in-his-favor-1848578203.html

(42) McLendon, Kim, "Polls show many millennial voters turning toward Trump if they can't have Sanders," *Inquisitr*, May 30, 2016, http://www.inquisitr.com/3146974/hillary-clinton-vs-donald-trump-polls-show-many-millennial-voters-turning-toward-trump-if-they-cant-have-sanders/

(43) Balz, Dan, "How Trump vs. Clinton could reshape the electoral map", *Washington Post*, May 28, 2016, https://www.washingtonpost.com/politics/how-trump-vs-clinton-would-reshape-the-electoral-map/2016/03/19/783a834c-ed35-11e5-b0fd-073d5930a7b7_story.html

(44) Scaramucci, Anthony, "The entrepreneur's case for Donald Trump," *Wall Street Journal*, May 16, 2016, http://www.wsj.com/articles/the-entrepreneurs-case-for-trump-1463344997

(45) Strassel, Kimberley A., "Opinion: Kimberley Strassel: Trump rakes the Clinton muck," *Wall Street Journal*, May 26, 2016, http://www.wsj.com/articles/trump-rakes-the-clinton-muck-1464302380

(46) Limbaugh, Rush, "Nationalism trumps conservatism," WND Exclusive, Jan. 20, 2016, http://www.wnd.com/2016/01/nationalism-trumps-conservatism-says-limbaugh/

(47) Long, Heather, "Clinton predicted to beat Trump...due to economics," CNN Money, May 26, 2016, http://money.cnn.com/2016/05/26/news/economy/hillary-clinton-beat-donald-trump-moodys/

(48) Reich, Robert, "Why Trump might win," *RealClearPolitics*, May 24, 2016, http://www.realclearpolitics.com/articles/2016/05/24/why_trump_might_win_130653.html

(49) "Rohit Sharma on Quora to the question if Donald Trump will win the US presidency," *Quora*, Feb. 4, 2016, https://www.quora.com/Is-Donald-Trump-likely-to-win-the-2016-election-late-2015-early-2016

(50) NCC Staff, "Historic re-election pattern doesn't favor Democrats in 2016," Constitution Center, Jan. 25, 2013, http://blog.constitutioncenter.org/2013/01/historic-re-election-pattern-doesnt-favor-democrats-in-2016/

CHAPTER 3: PRESIDENT TRUMP

(1) Benac, Nancy, "Trump has lived his life as one long negotiation going with his gut and winging it when necessary," *US News & World Report*, Apr. 4, 2016, http://www.usnews.com/news/politics/articles/2016-04-04/imagining-a-trump-administration-count-on-unpredictability

(2) Latimer, Matt, "Trump—the first 100 days," *Politico*, Feb. 26, 2016, http://www.politico.com/magazine/story/2016/02/donald-trump-2016-213677

(3) Luttwak, N. Edward, "Suffering from Trumphobia? Get over it," *Wall Street Journal*, Mar. 9, 2016, http://www.wsj.com/articles/suffering-from-trumphobia-get-over-it-1457565216

(4) Scaramucci, Anthony, "The entrepreneur's case for Trump," *Wall Street Journal*, May 15, 2016, http://www.wsj.com/articles/the-entrepreneurs-case-for-trump-1463344997

(5) Benac, Nancy, "Trump has lived his life as one long negotiation going with his gut and winging it when necessary," *US News & World Report*, Apr. 4, 2016, http://www.usnews.com/news/politics/articles/2016-04-04/imagining-a-trump-administration-count-on-unpredictability

(6) Griswold, Alex, "CBS's John Dickerson: Hillary Clinton is more vindictive than Donald Trump," Mediaite, May 20, 2016, http://www.mediaite.com/election-2016/cbss-john-dickerson-hillary-clinton-is-more-vindictive-than-donald-trump/

(7) D'Antonio, Michael, *Never enough*, 2015, Thomas Dunne Books, St. Martin's Press, p. 179

(8) D'Antonio, Michael, *Never enough*, 2015, Thomas Dunne Books, St. Martin's Press, p. 226

(9) D'Antonio, Michael, *Never enough*, 2015, Thomas Dunne Books, St. Martin's Press, p. 152–153

(10) D'Antonio, Michael, *Never enough*, 2015, Thomas Dunne Books, St. Martin's Press, pp. 154–55

(11) Sobieraj, Sandra and Triggs, Charlotte, "Who is the real Donald Trump?", People Magazine April 11, 2016, http://www.people.com/article/real-donald-trump-people-special-report

(12) D'Antonio, Michael, "Never Enough", p. 117-118, 2015, Thomas Dunne Books, St. Martin's Press

(13) Gulbis, Natalie, "The Donald Trump I know", Golf. com, June 2nd, 2016, http://www.golf.com/tour-and-news/ natalie-gulbis-donald-trump-i-know?xid=nl_news

(14) D'Antonio, Michael, "Never Enough", p. 264, 2015, Thomas Dunne Books, St. Martin's Press

(15) Huntsman, M. Jon Jr. and Lieberman, Joe, "Stop fighting, start fixing," *Fortune*, May 1, 2016, https://www.nolabels.org/ ideas/#ideas-menu-intro

(16) Donald Trump's website, June 27, 2016, https://www.donaldjtrump. com/positions/tax-reform

(17) Rubin, Richard, "US companies are stashing $2.1 trillion overseas to avoid taxes," *Bloomberg*, March 4, 2015, http://www.bloomberg.com/news/articles/2015-03-04/u-s-companies-are-stashing-2-1-trillion-overseas-to-avoid-taxes

(18) "Fear trumps hope," *Economist*, May 7–13, 2016, pp. 20–22

(19) Cuban, Mark, "Some thoughts on the presidential race and socio-capitalism", blogmaverick.com, Feb. 8, 2016, http://blogmaverick. com/2016/02/08/some-thoughts-on-the-presidential-race-and-socio-capitalism/Cuban, Mark, Cyber Dust, blogmaverick.com

(20) Trump, Donald, "Crippled America," 2015, p. 20, Simon and Schuster

(21) Donald Trump's website, June 27, 2016, https://www.donaldjtrump. com/positions/pay-for-the-wall

(22) Donald Trump's website, June 27, 2016, https://www.donaldjtrump. com/positions/immigration-reform

(23) Donald Trump's website, June 27, 2016, https://www.donaldjtrump. com/positions/healthcare-reform

(24) Donald Trump's website, June 27, 2016, https://www.donaldjtrump. com/positions/second-amendment-rights

(25) D'Antonio, Michael, *Never enough*, 2015, Thomas Dunne Books, St. Martin's Press, pp. 181–83

(26) "Rumsfeld: Why I will vote for Donald Trump", Fox News, Online June 22, 2016, http://www.foxnews.com/transcript/2016/06/22/rumsfeld-why-will-vote-for-trump/

(27) Parton, Digby, "The most fearsome hawk of all: Donald Trump's careless, brutal plans for the US puts the world in peril," *Salon*, May 31, 2016, http://www.salon.com/2016/05/31/the_most_fearsome_hawk_of_all_donald_trumps_careless_brutal_plans_for_the_u_s_puts_the_world_in_peril/

(28) Donald Trump's website, June 27, 2009, https://www.donaldjtrump.com/press-releases/donald-j.-trump-foreign-policy-speech

(29) Coll, Steve, "Global Trump," *New Yorker*, Apr. 11, 2016, http://www.newyorker.com/magazine/2016/04/11/global-trump

(30) Lippman, Daniel, "The Economist rates Trump presidency among its top 10 global risks," *Politico*, Mar. 16, 2016, http://www.politico.com/story/2016/03/economist-trump-presidency-global-risk-220887

Chapter 4: Trump's Impact and Legacy

(1) Sirota, David, "Donald Trump echoes Ross Perot's anti-insider rhetoric, expands his white male base," *IBTimes*, Mar. 2, 2016, http://www.ibtimes.com/political-capital/donald-trump-echoes-ross-perots-anti-insider-rhetoric-expands-his-white-male-base

(2) Cooper, Matthew, "World under President Donald Trump," *Newsweek*, Mar. 25, 2016, http://www.newsweek.com/2016/03/25/world-under-president-donald-trump-437158.html

(3) Cassidy, John, "A Europe of Donald Trumps?" *New Yorker*, May 2, 2016, http://www.newyorker.com/news/john-cassidy/a-europe-of-donald-trumps

(4) *Wikipedia*, "Populism,", June 27, 2016, https://en.wikipedia.org/wiki/Populism

Made in the USA
Middletown, DE
15 September 2018